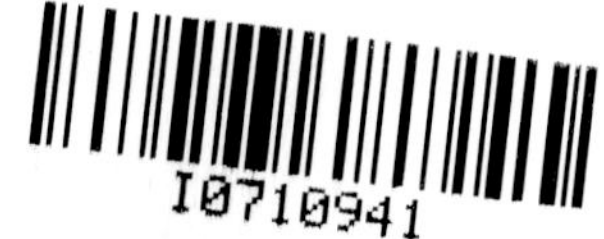

Happy Valentine's Day

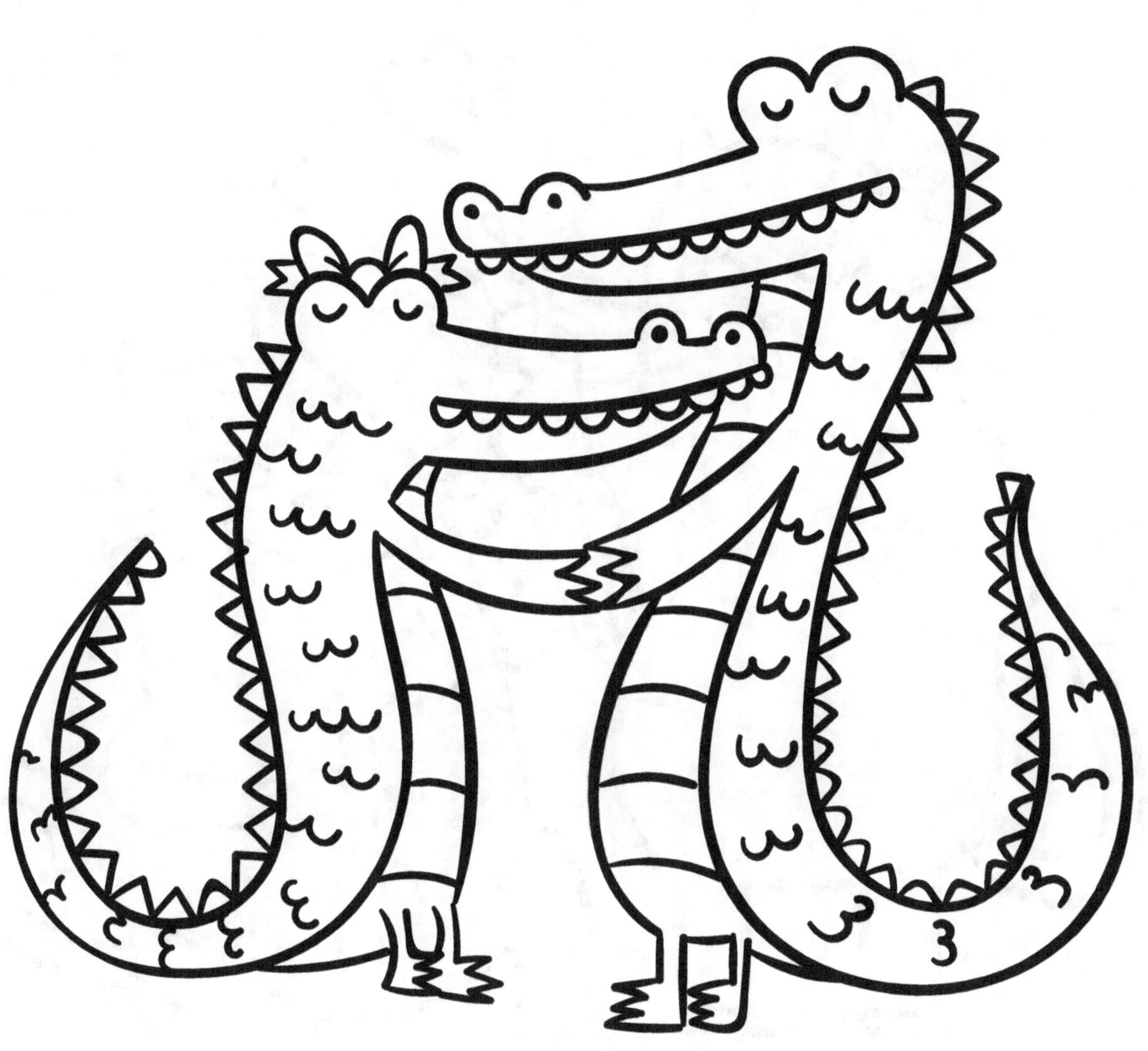

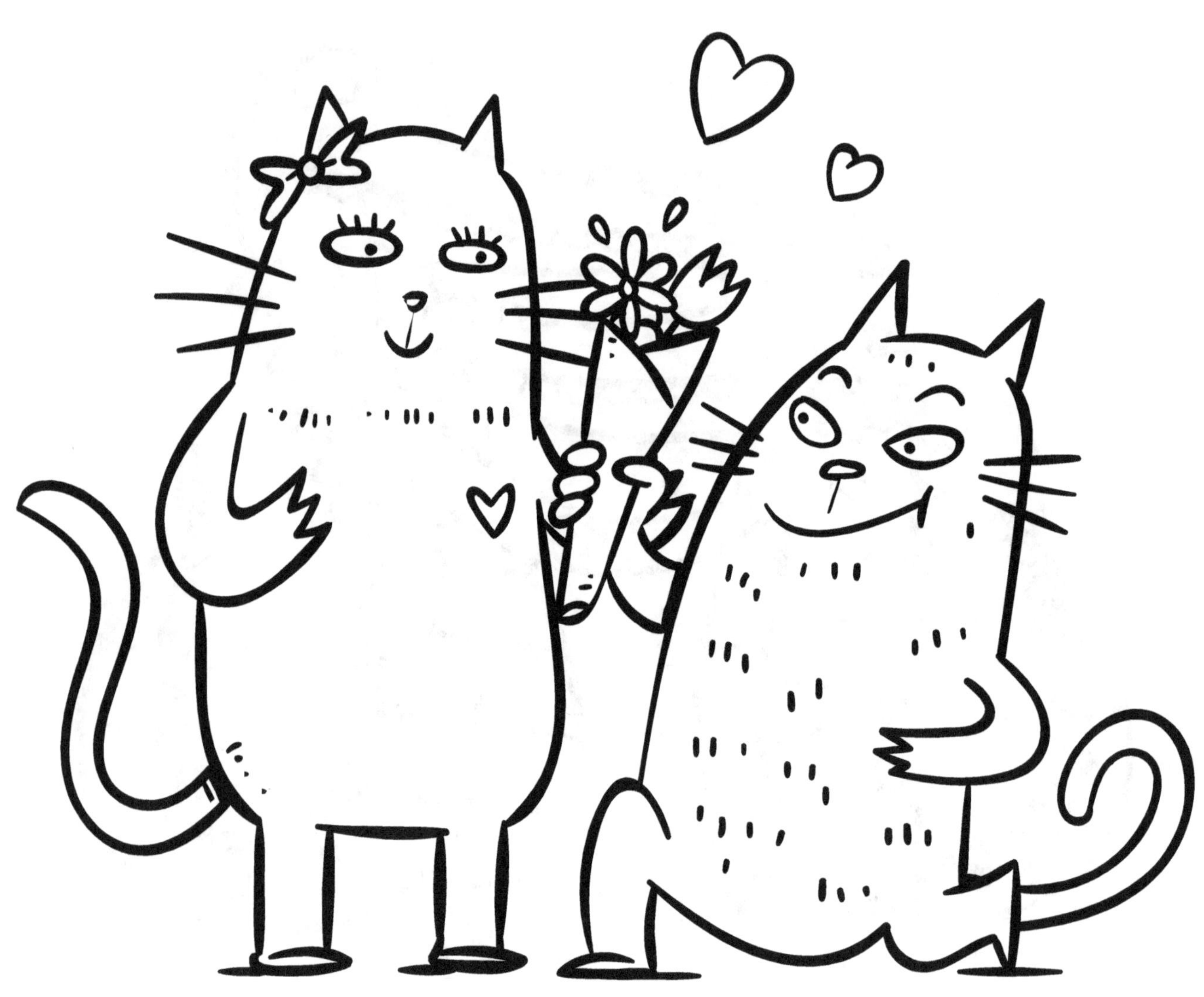

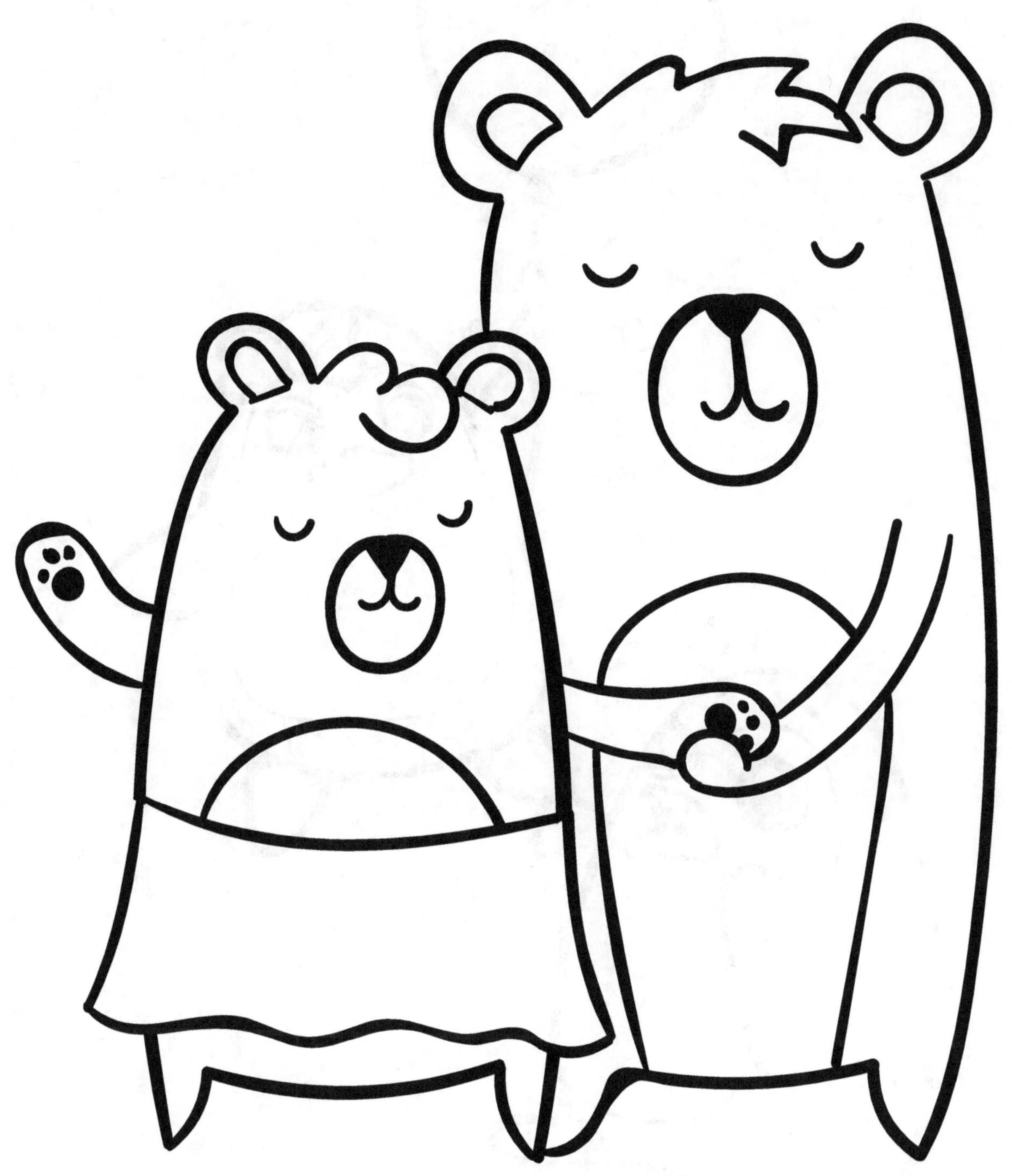

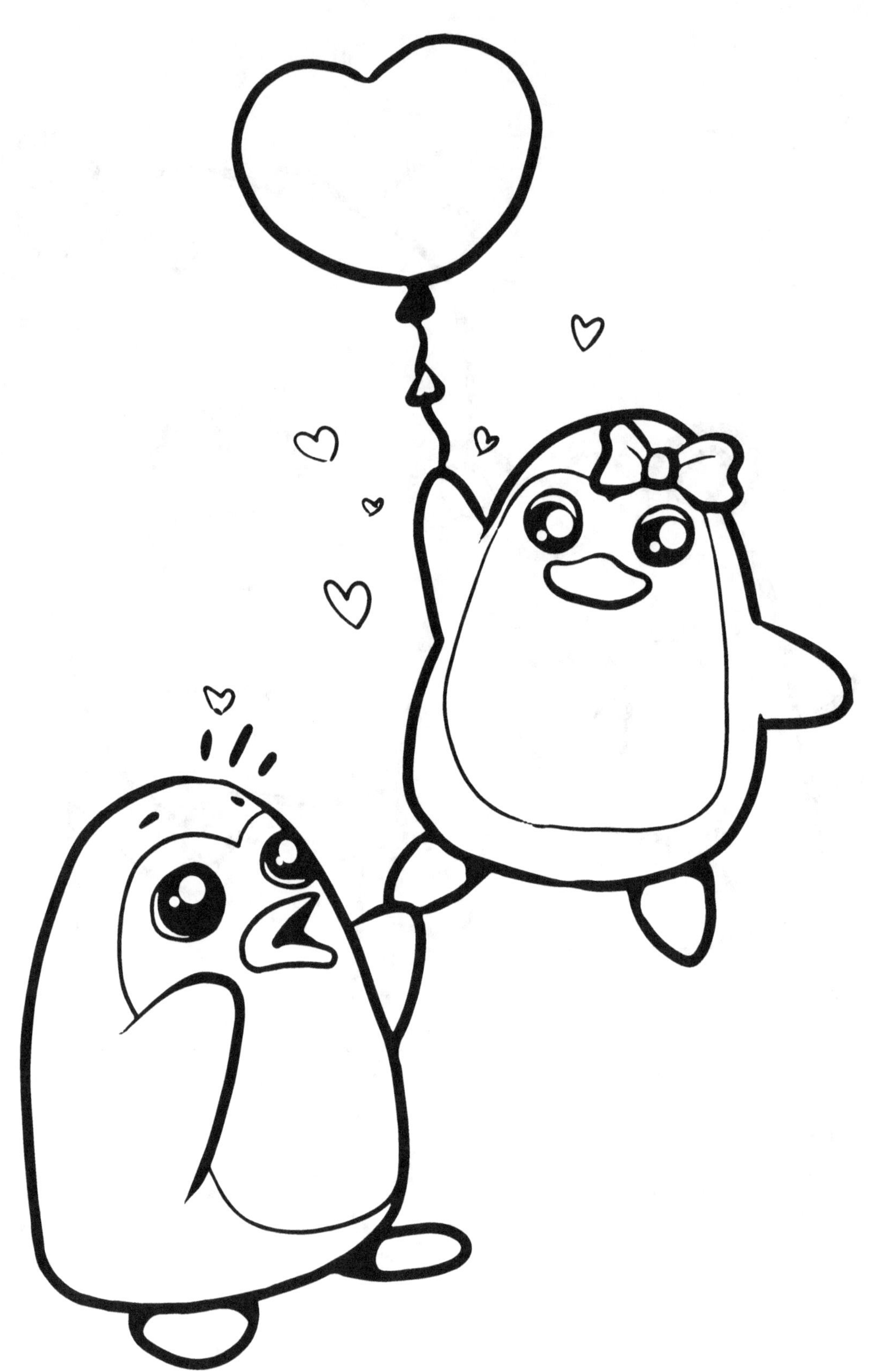

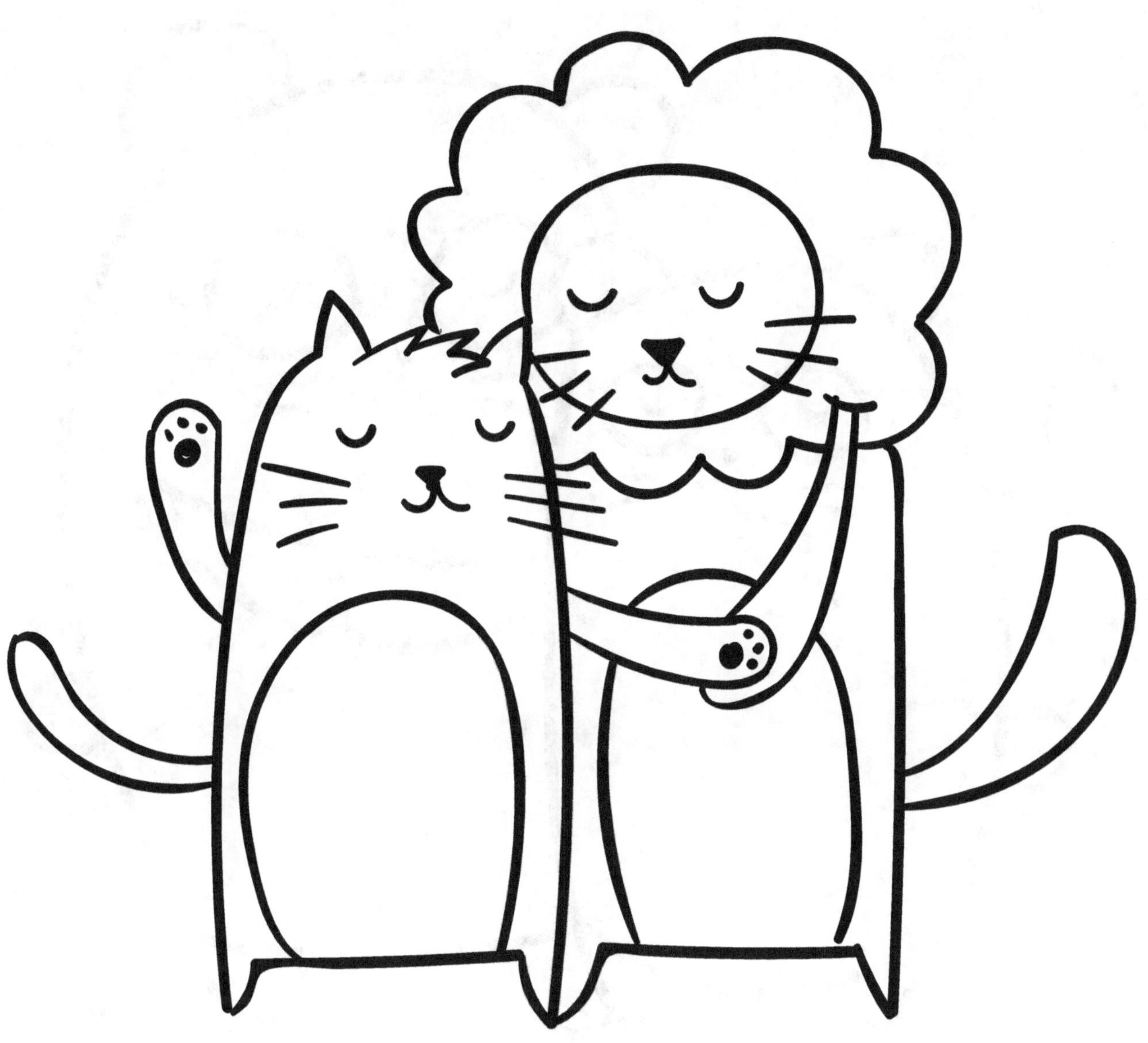

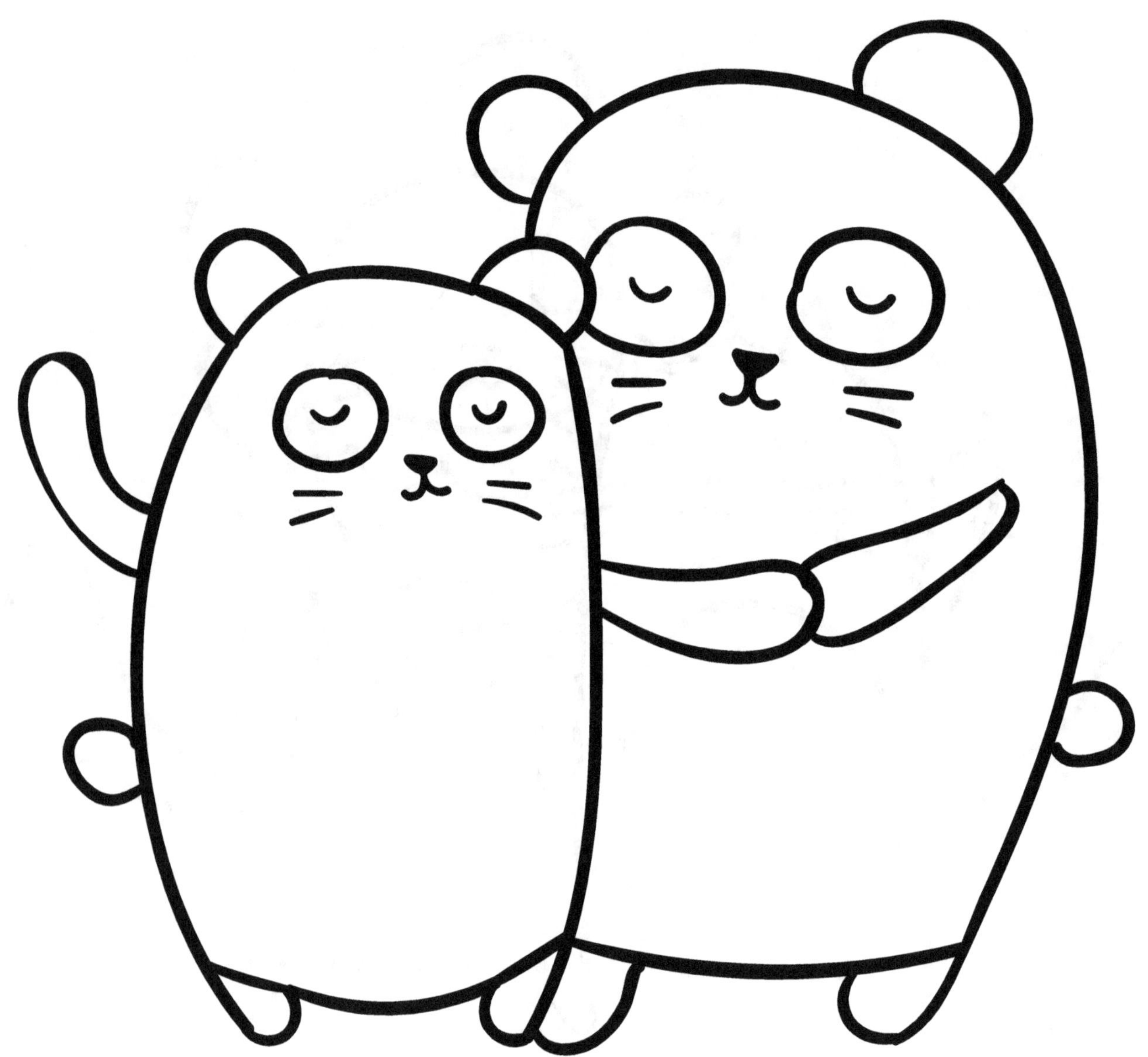

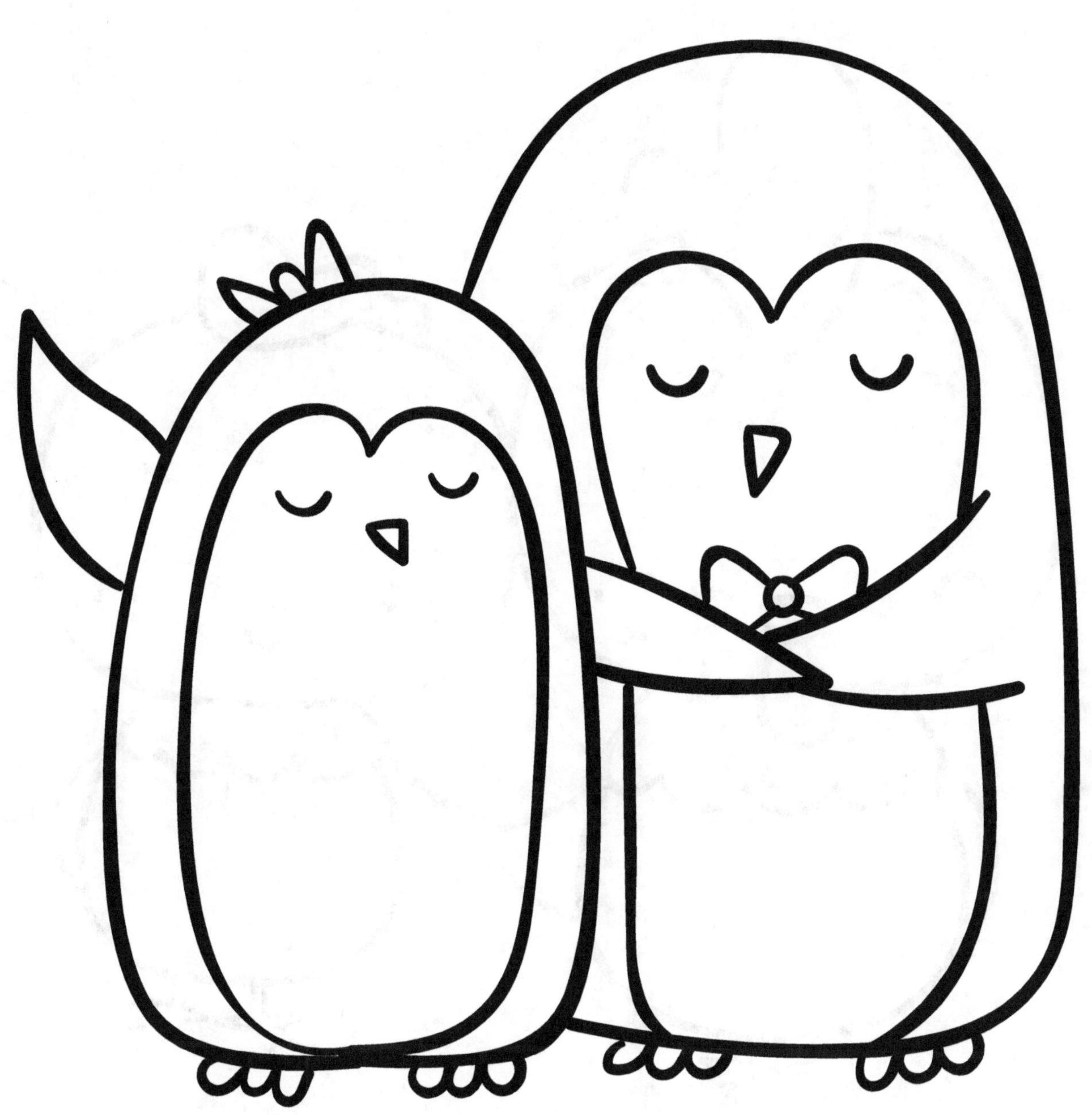

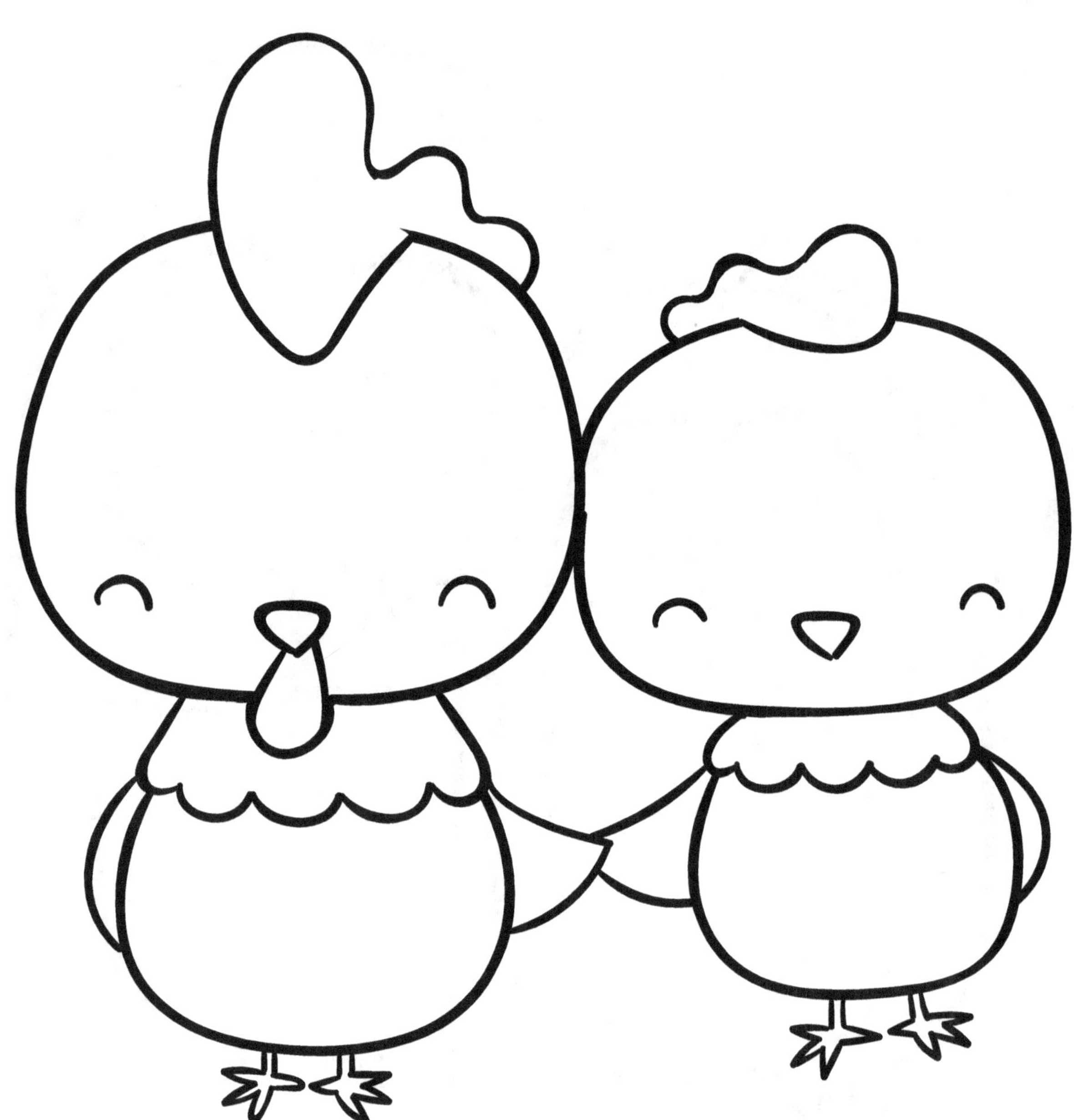

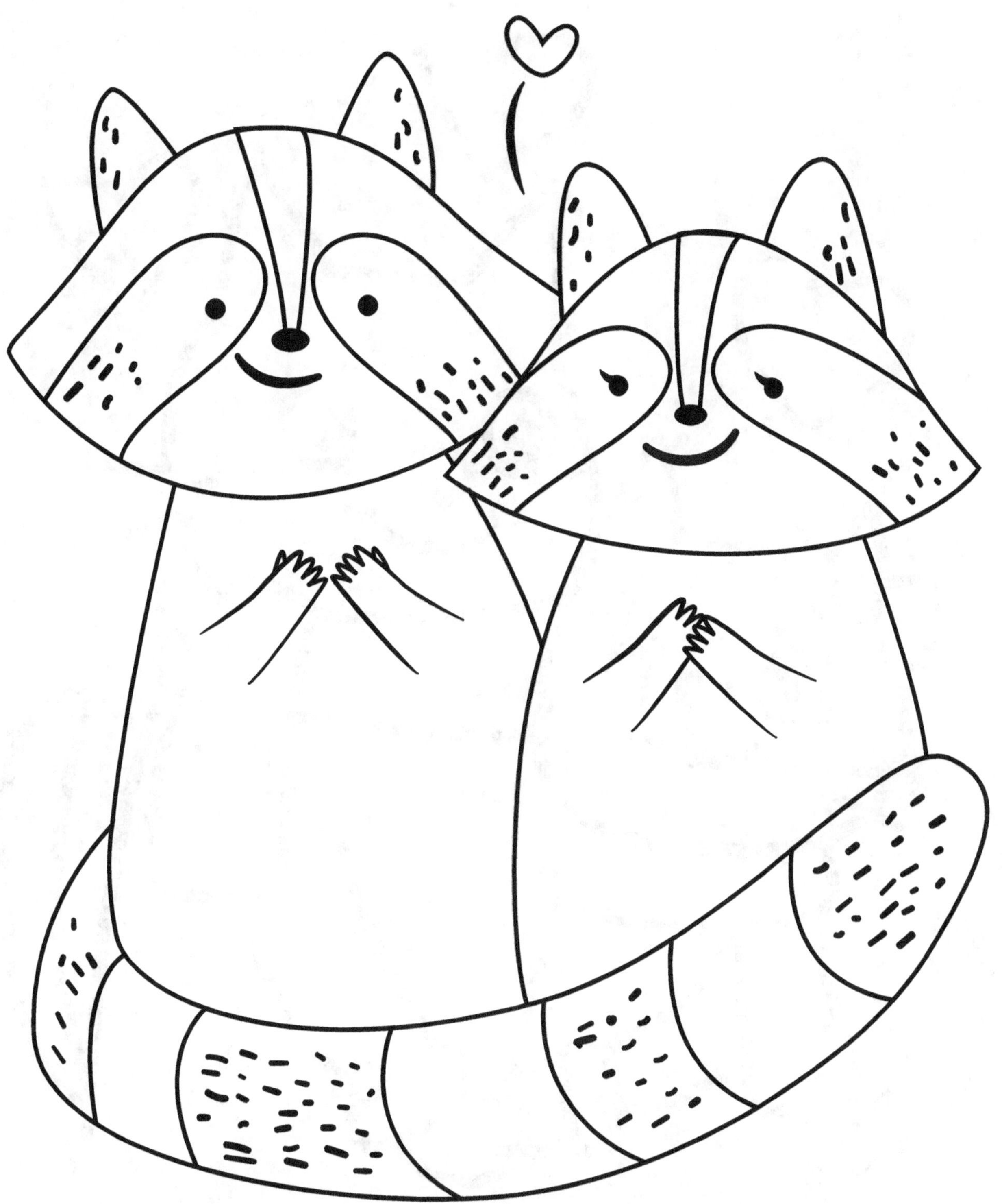

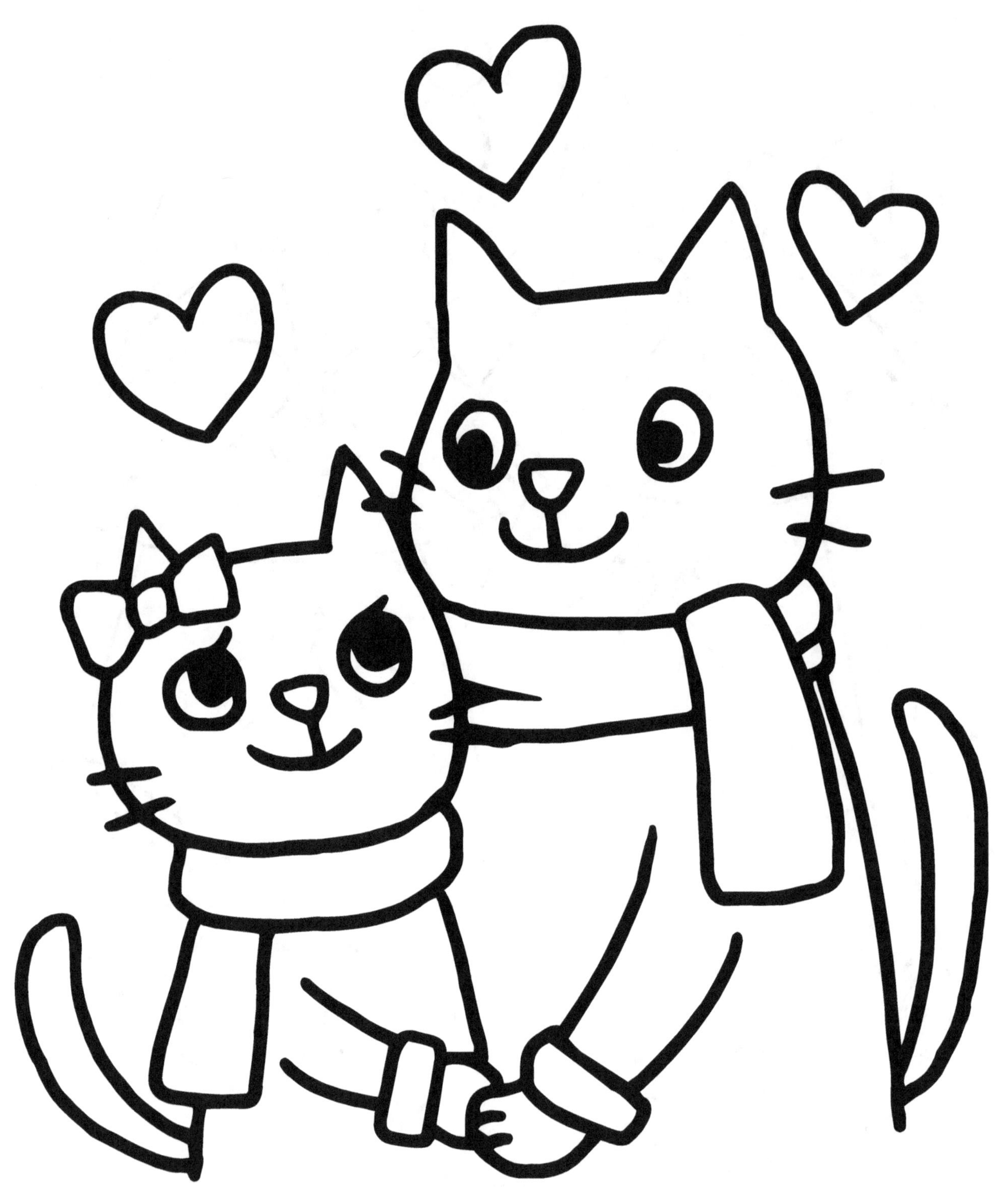

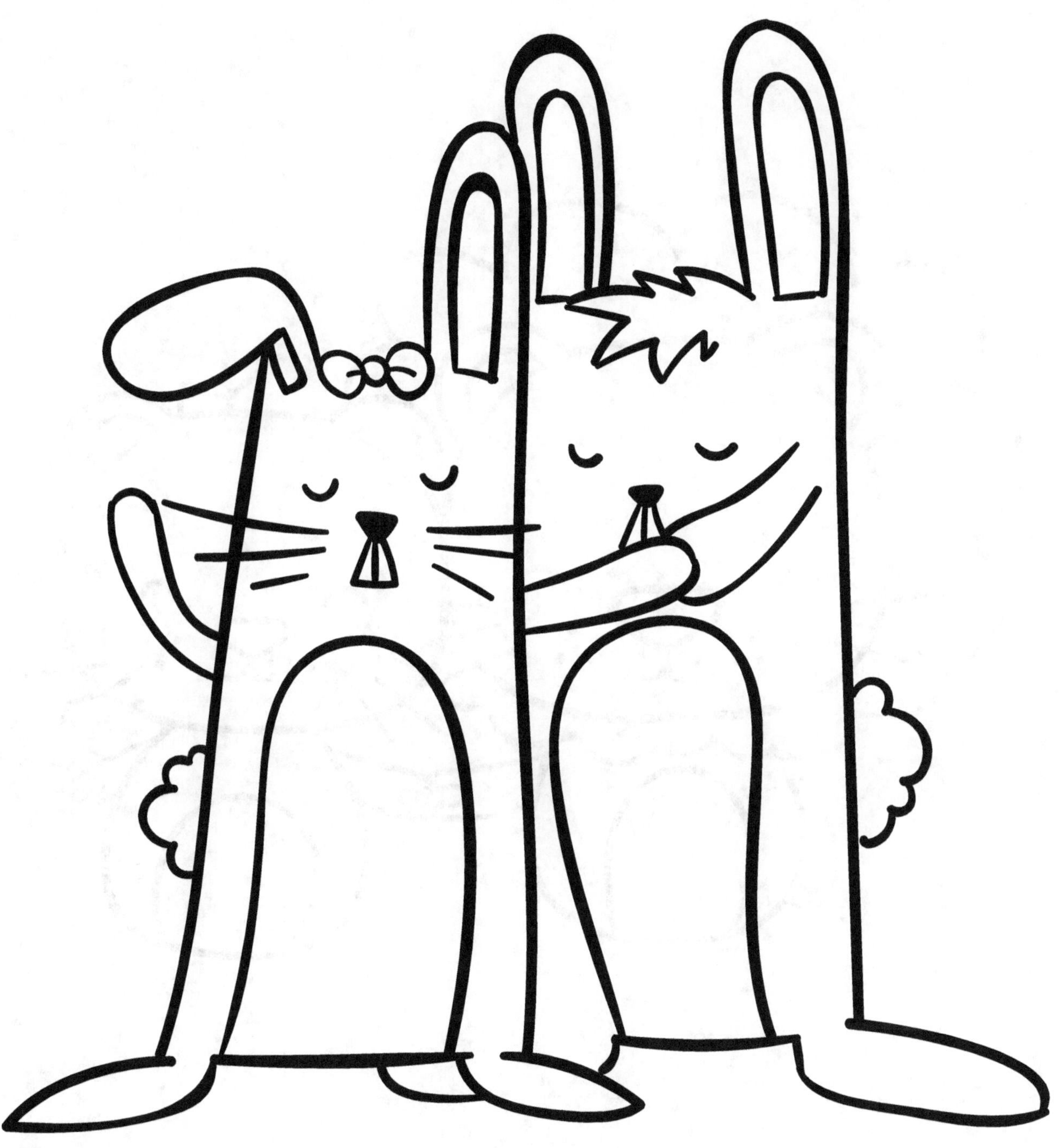

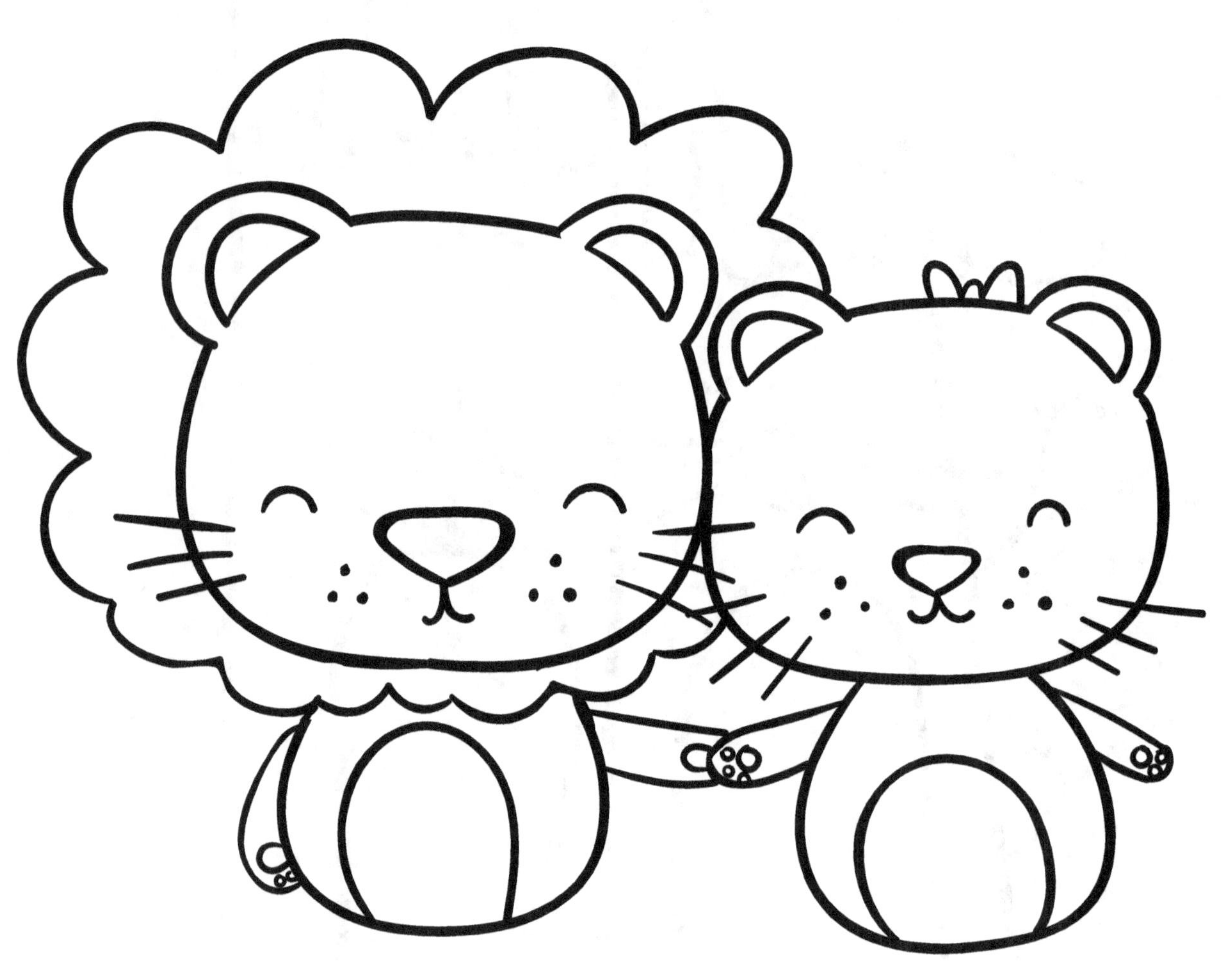

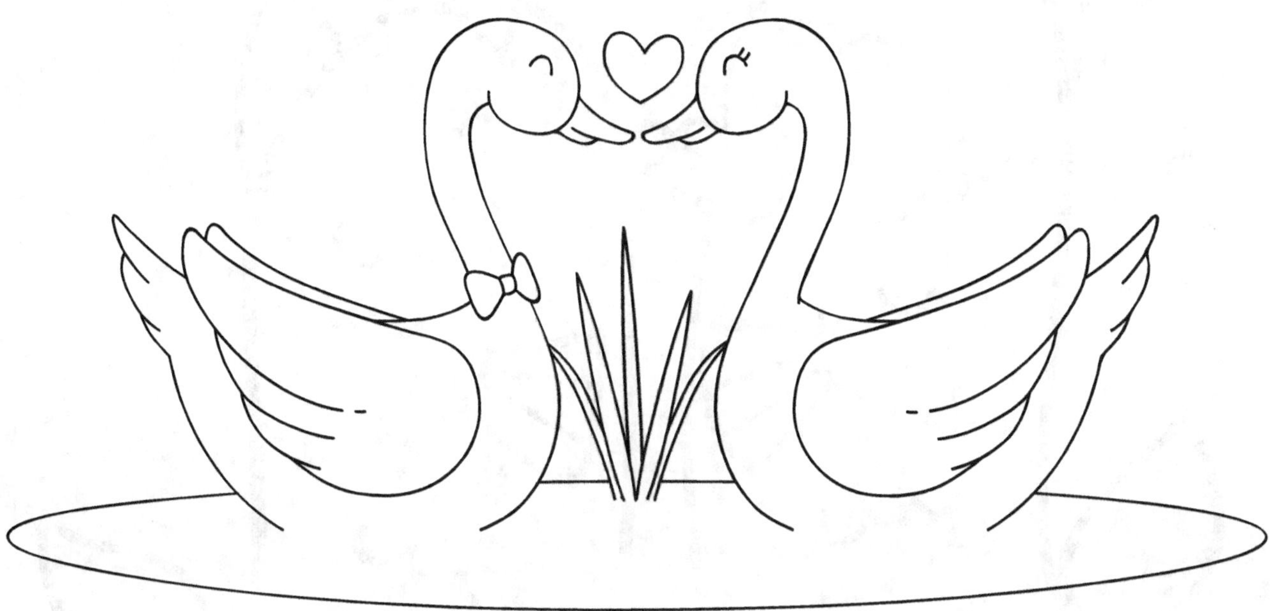

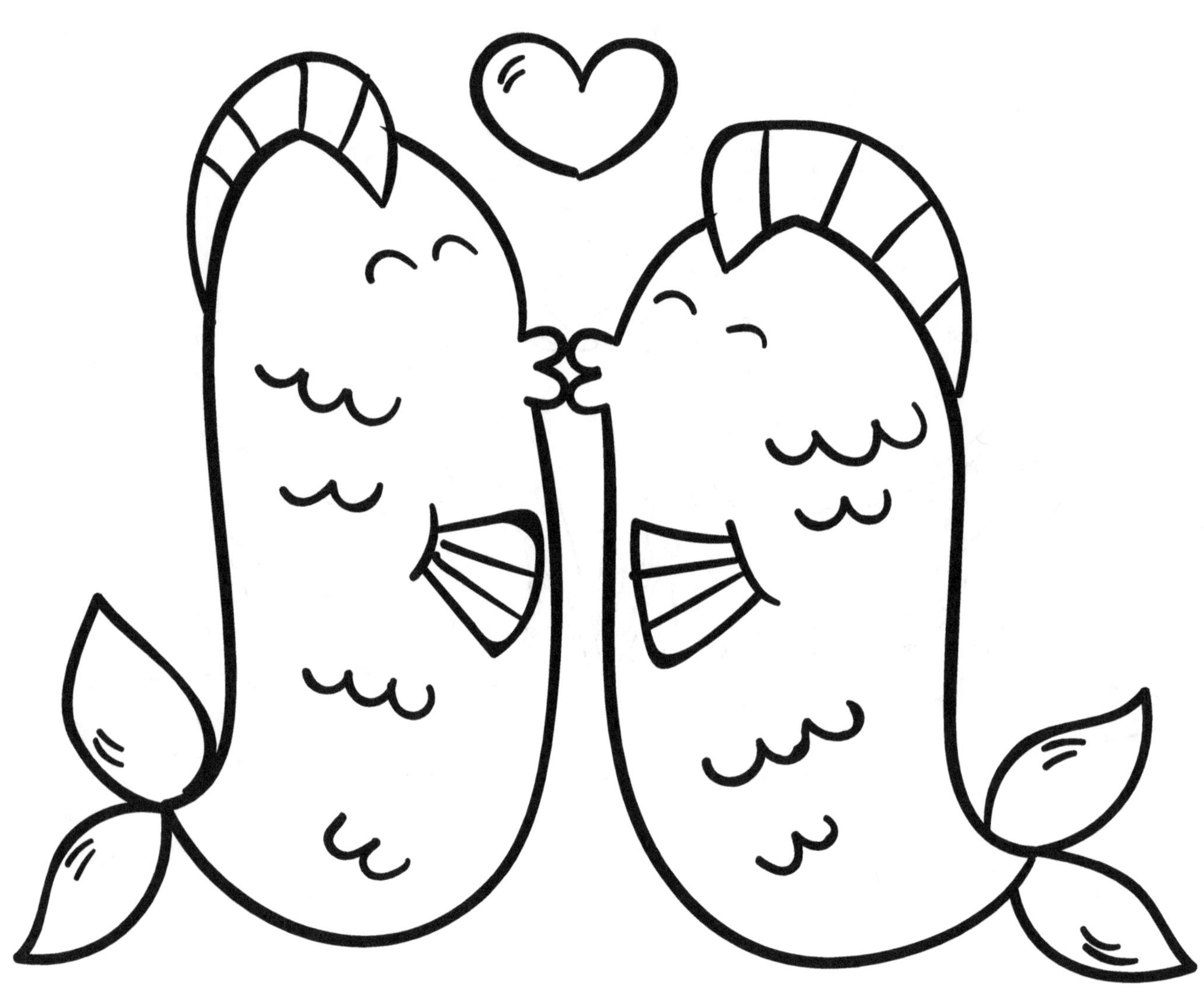

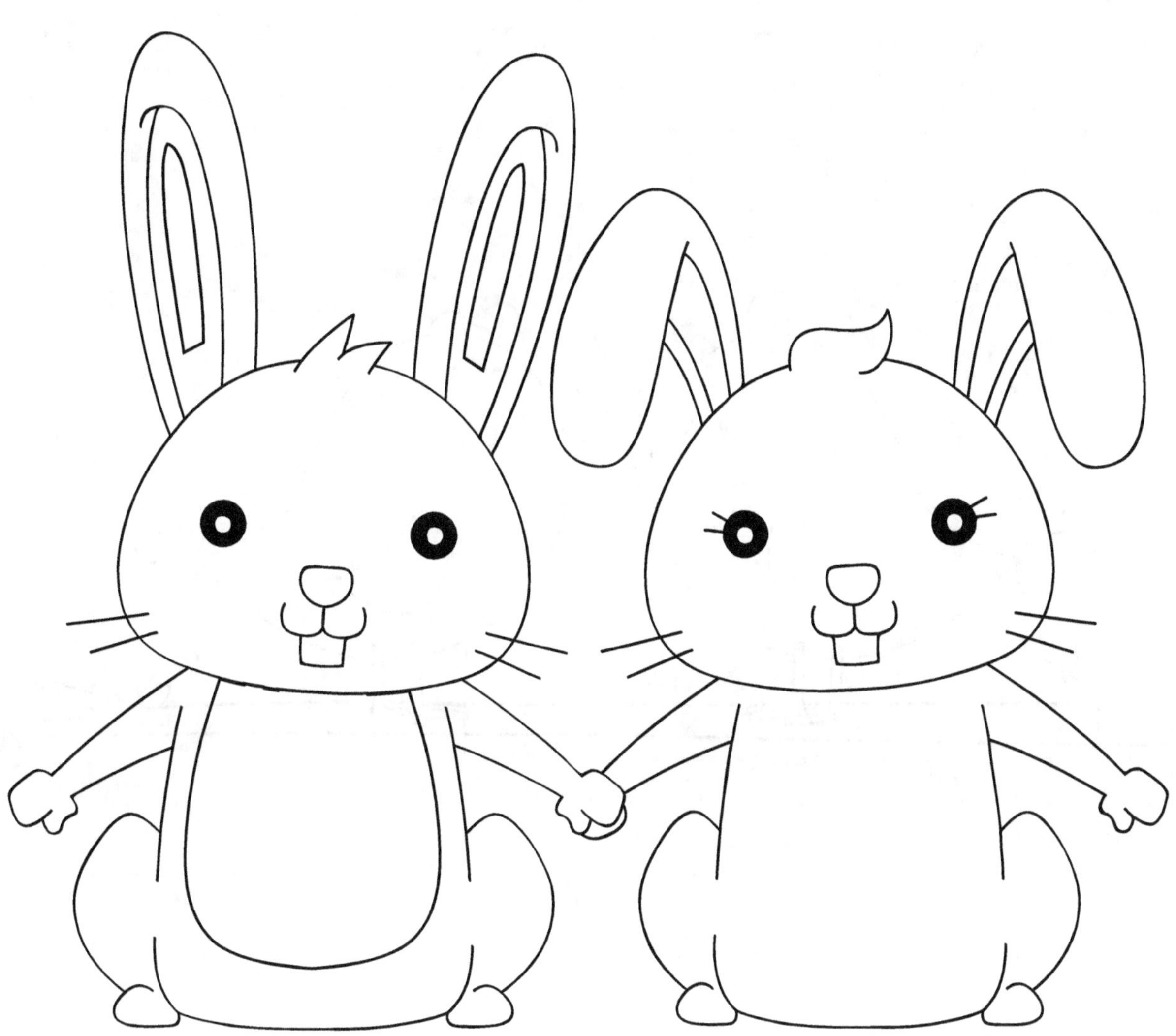

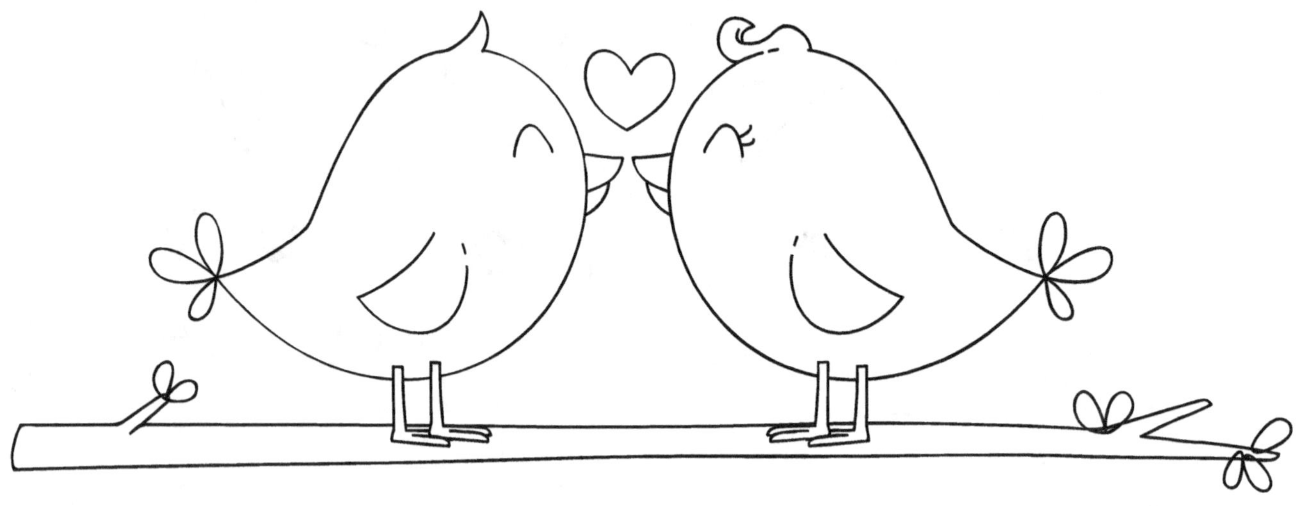

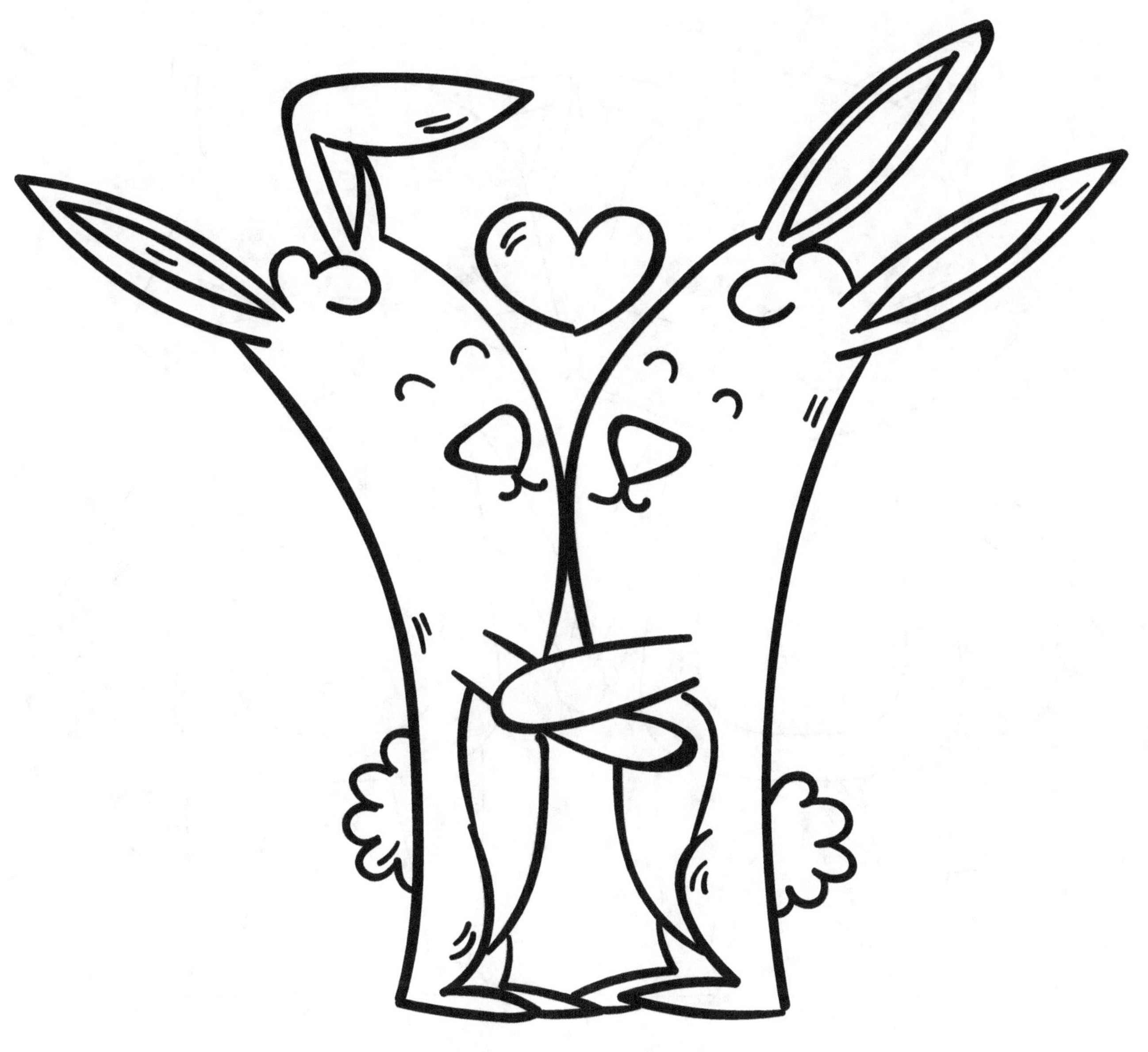

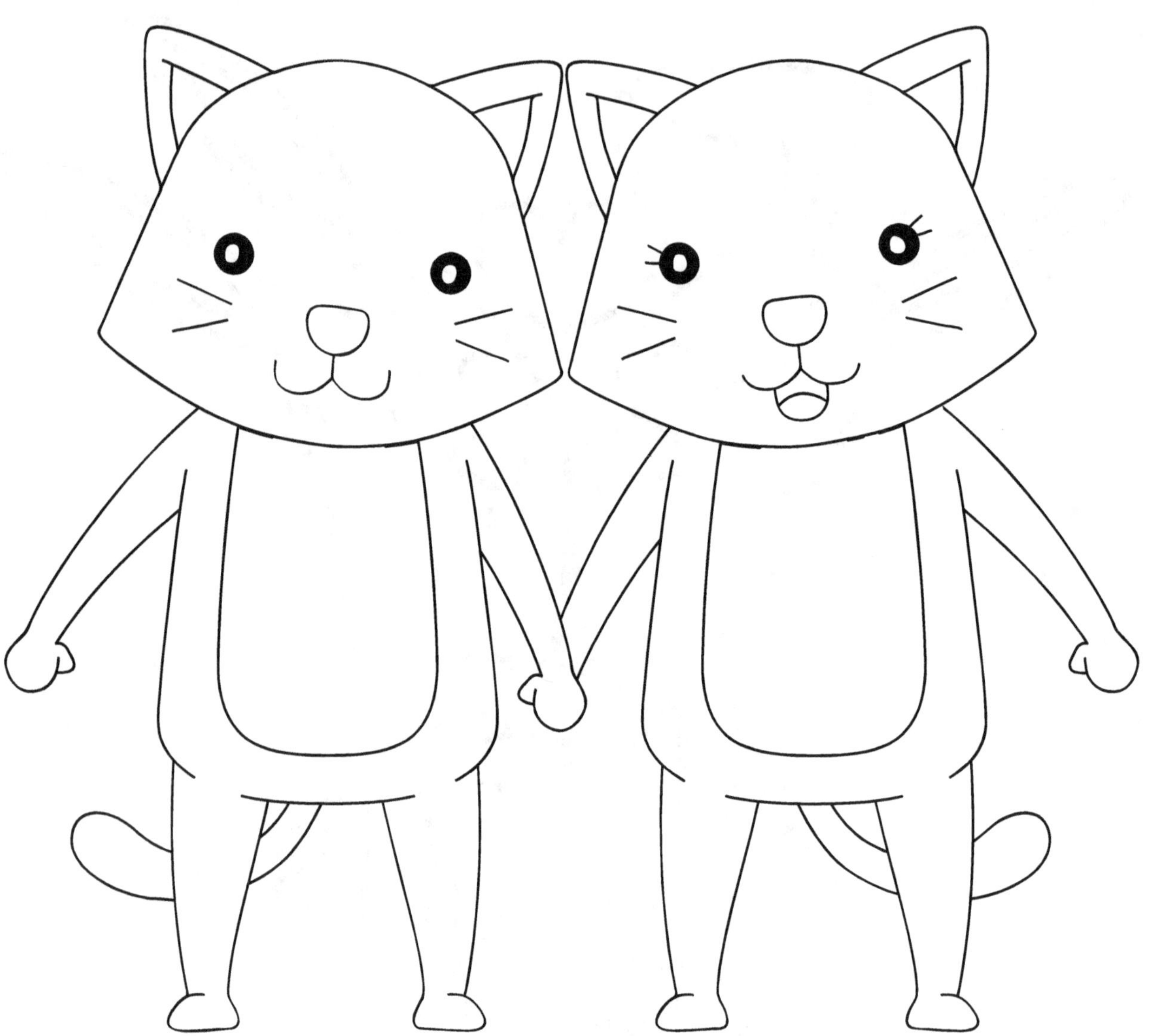

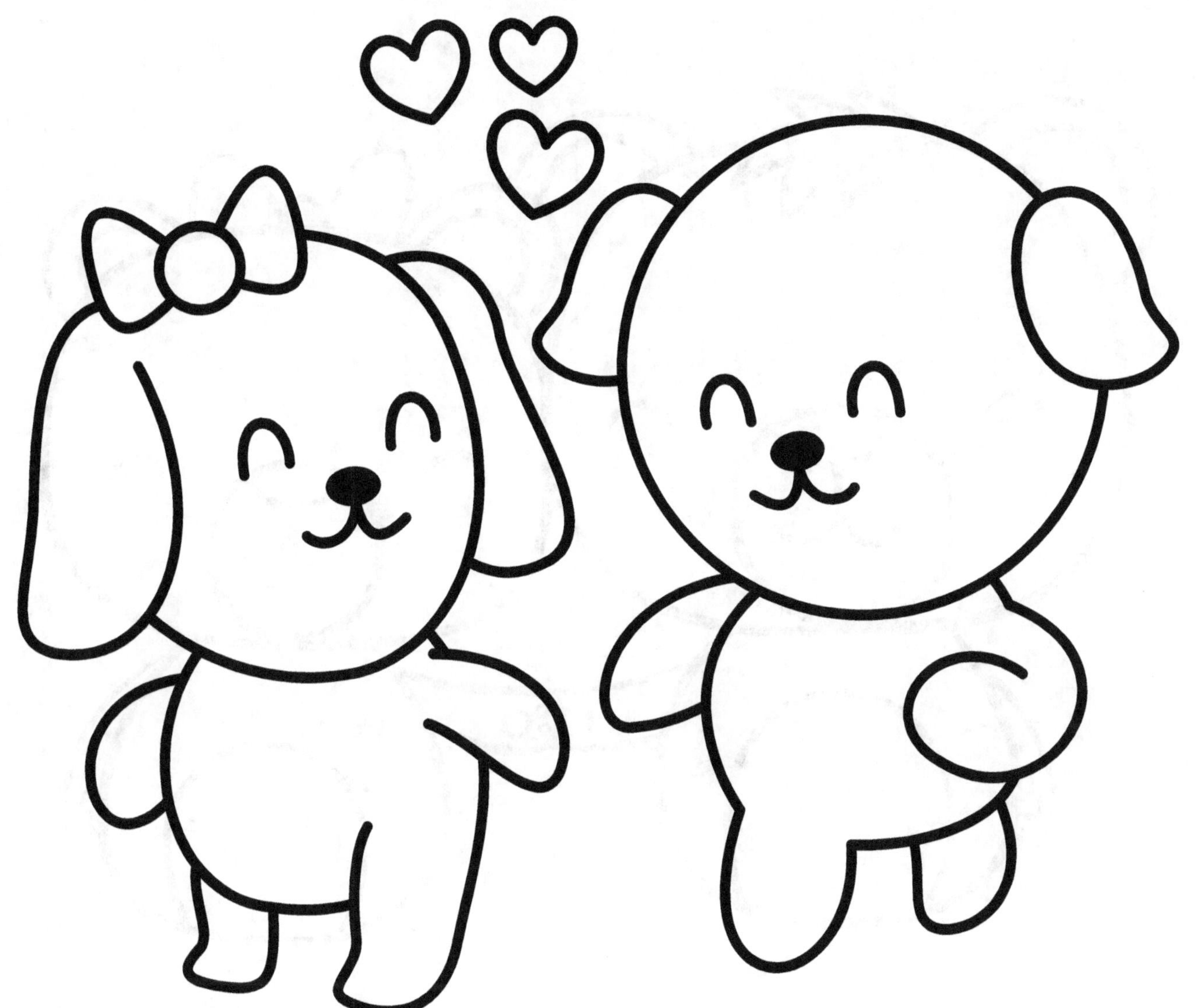

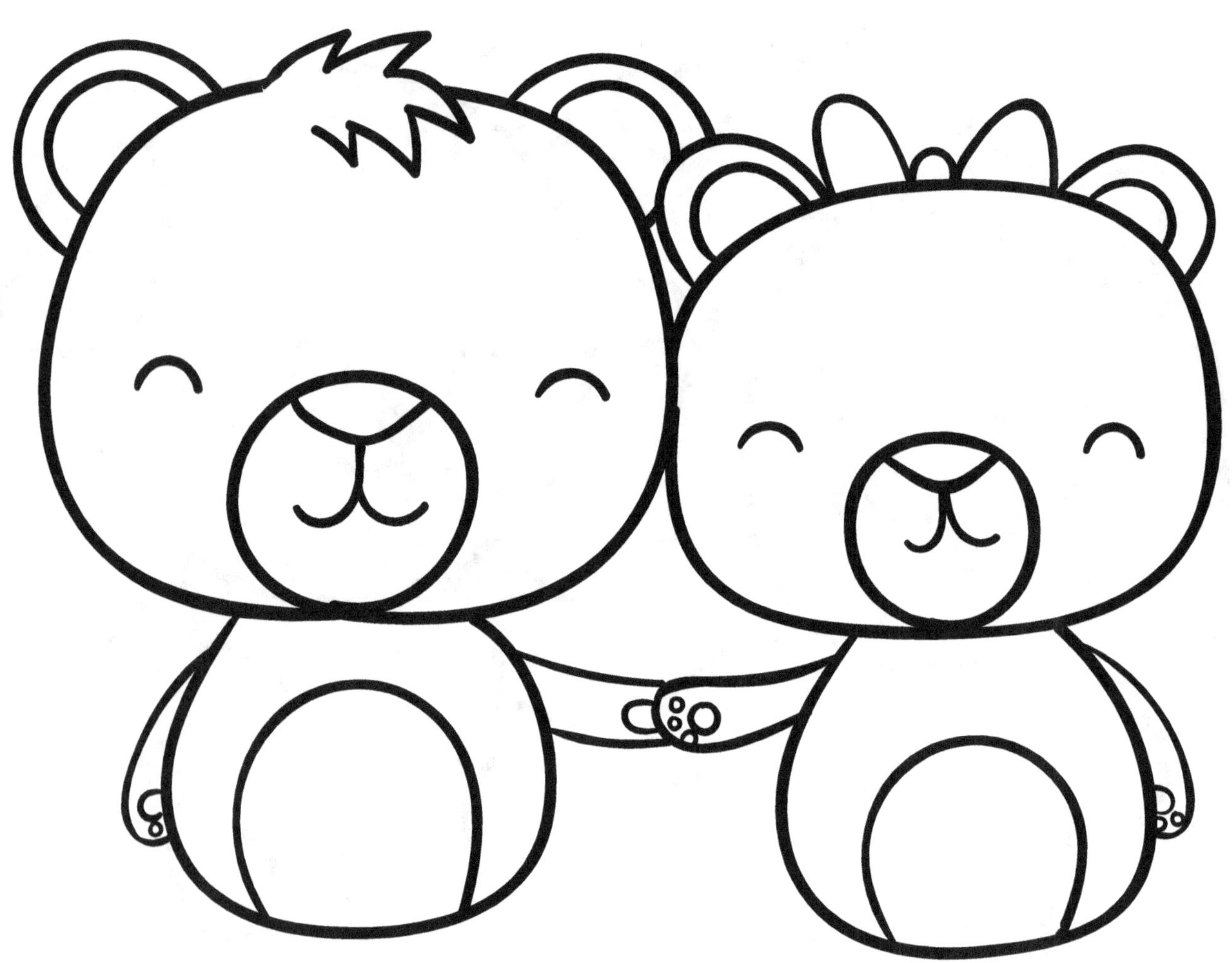

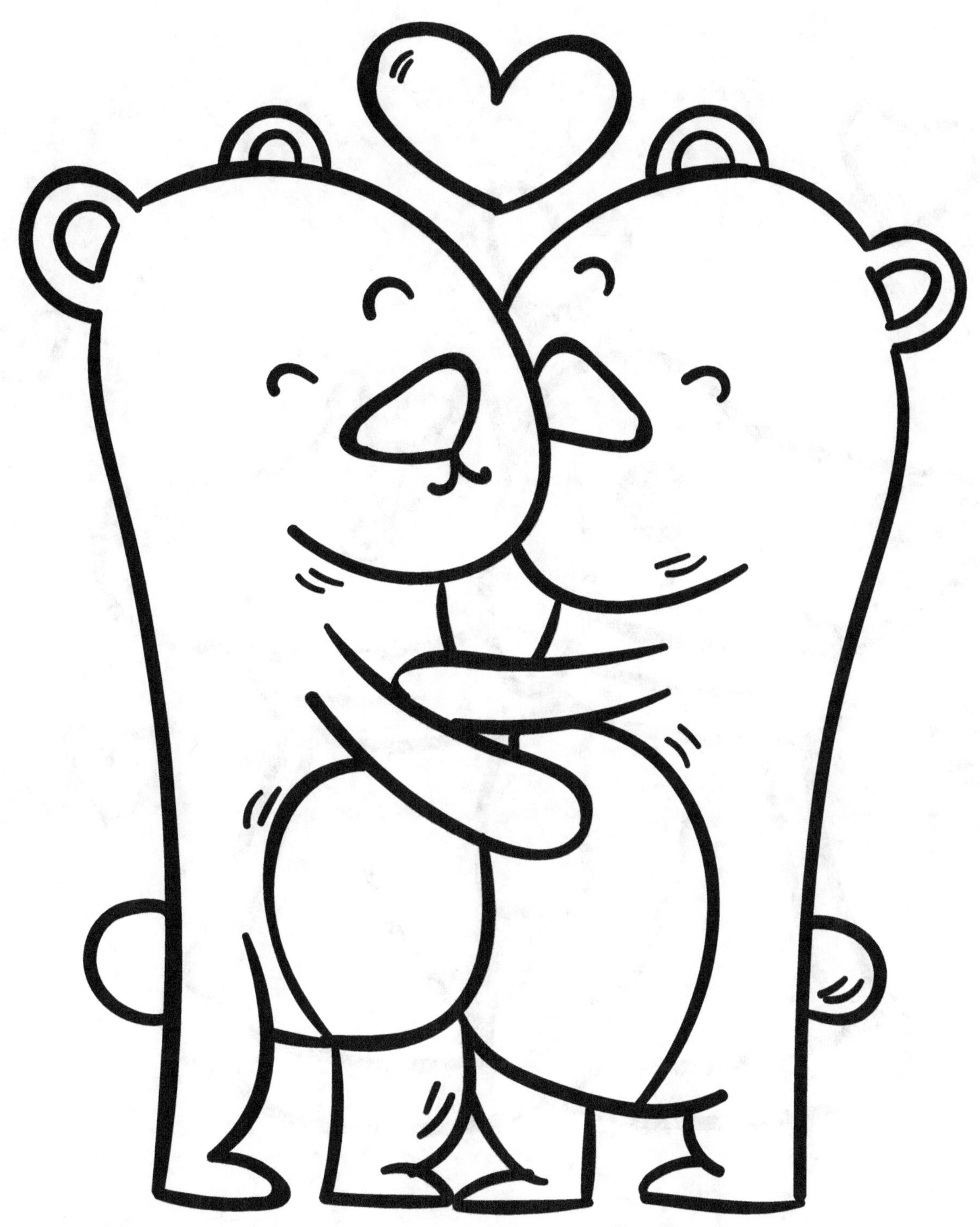

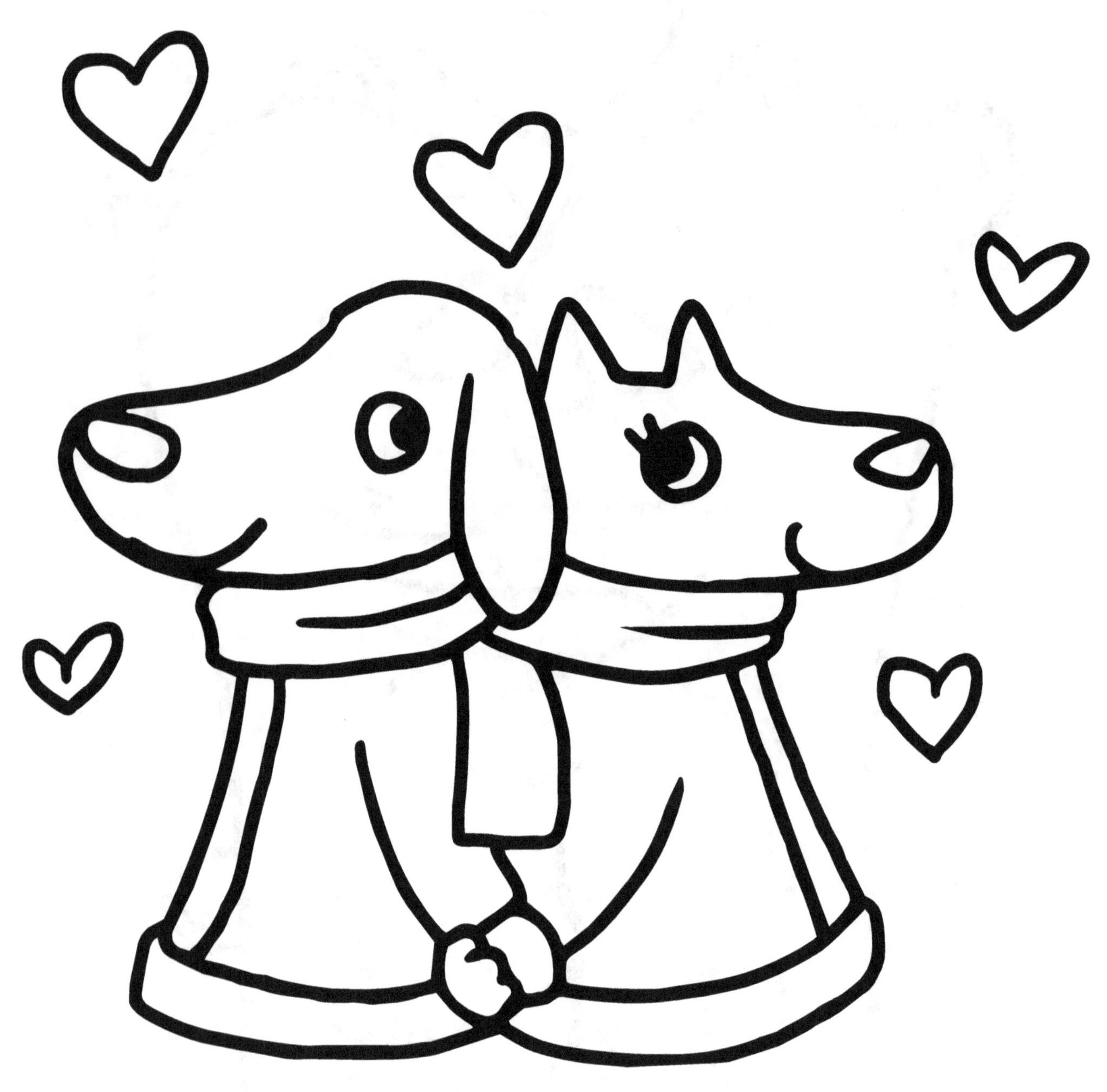

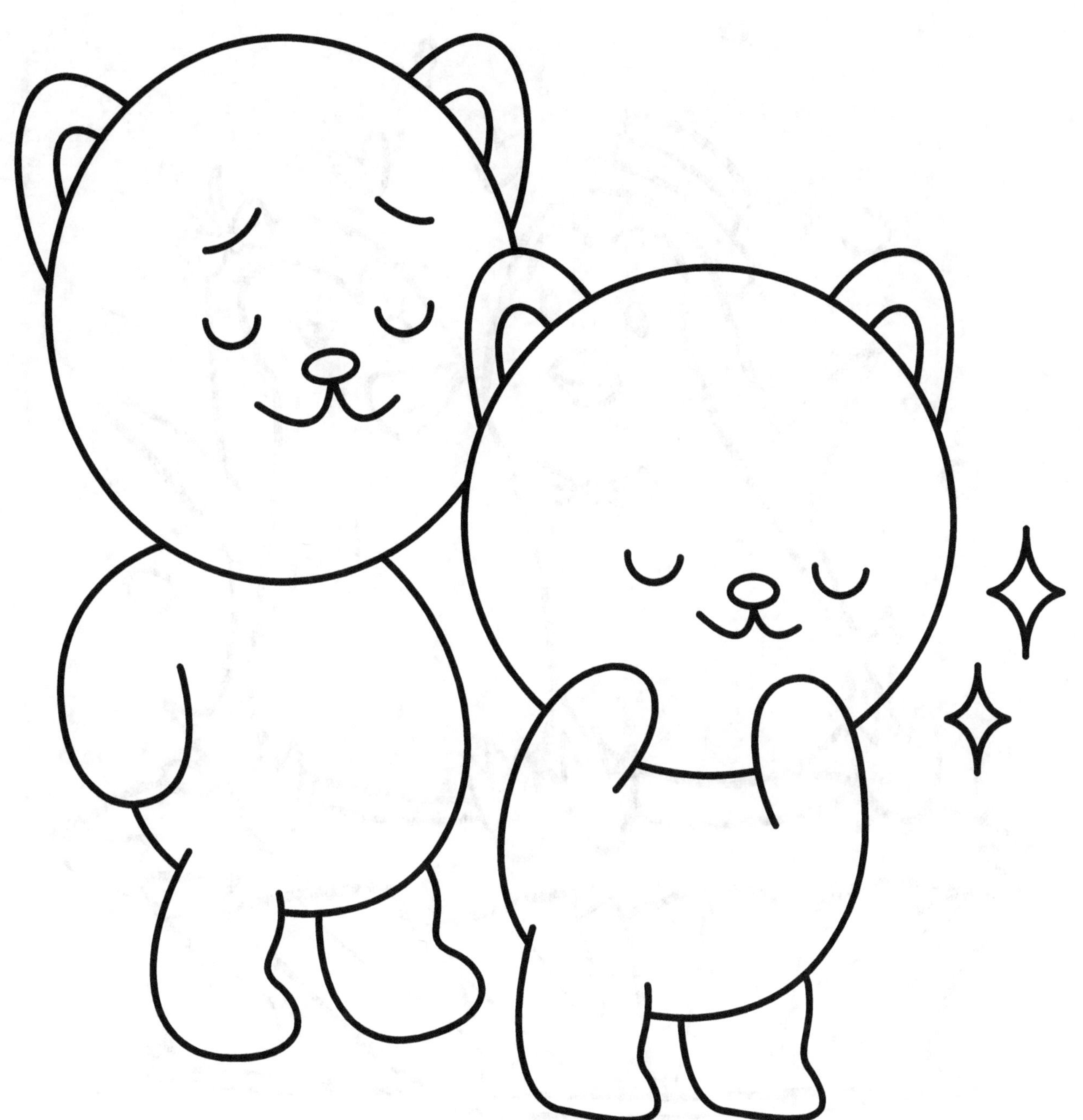

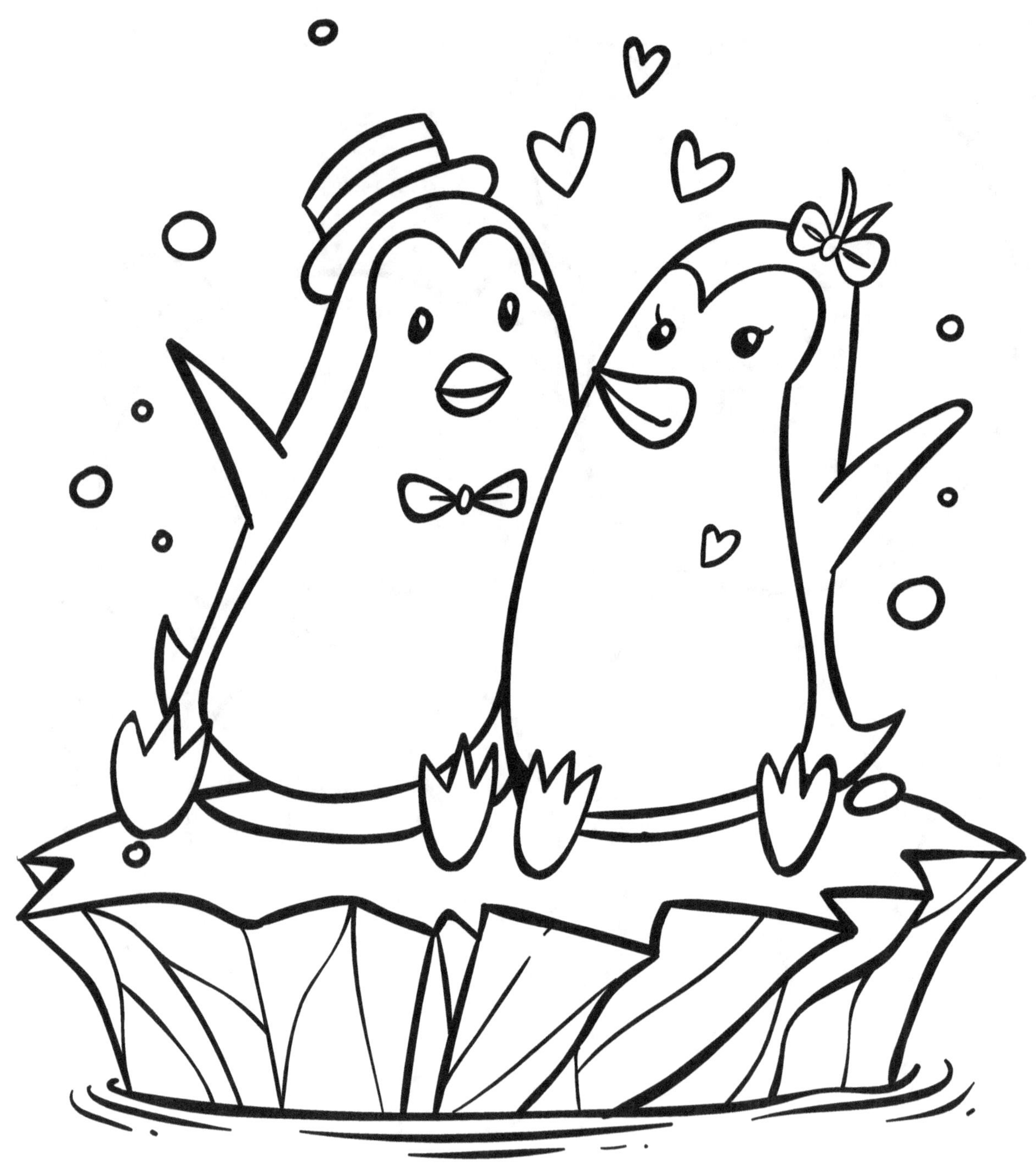

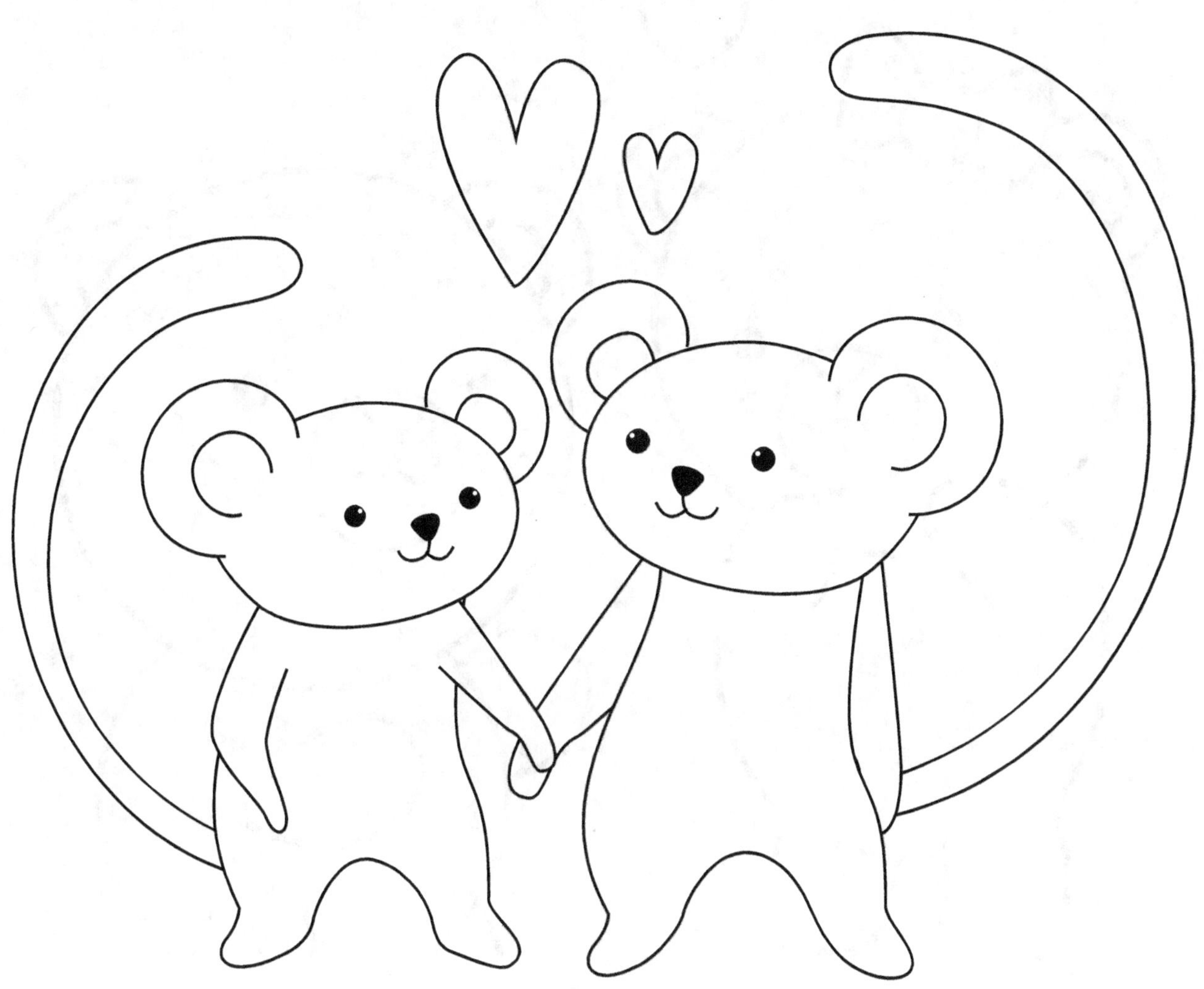

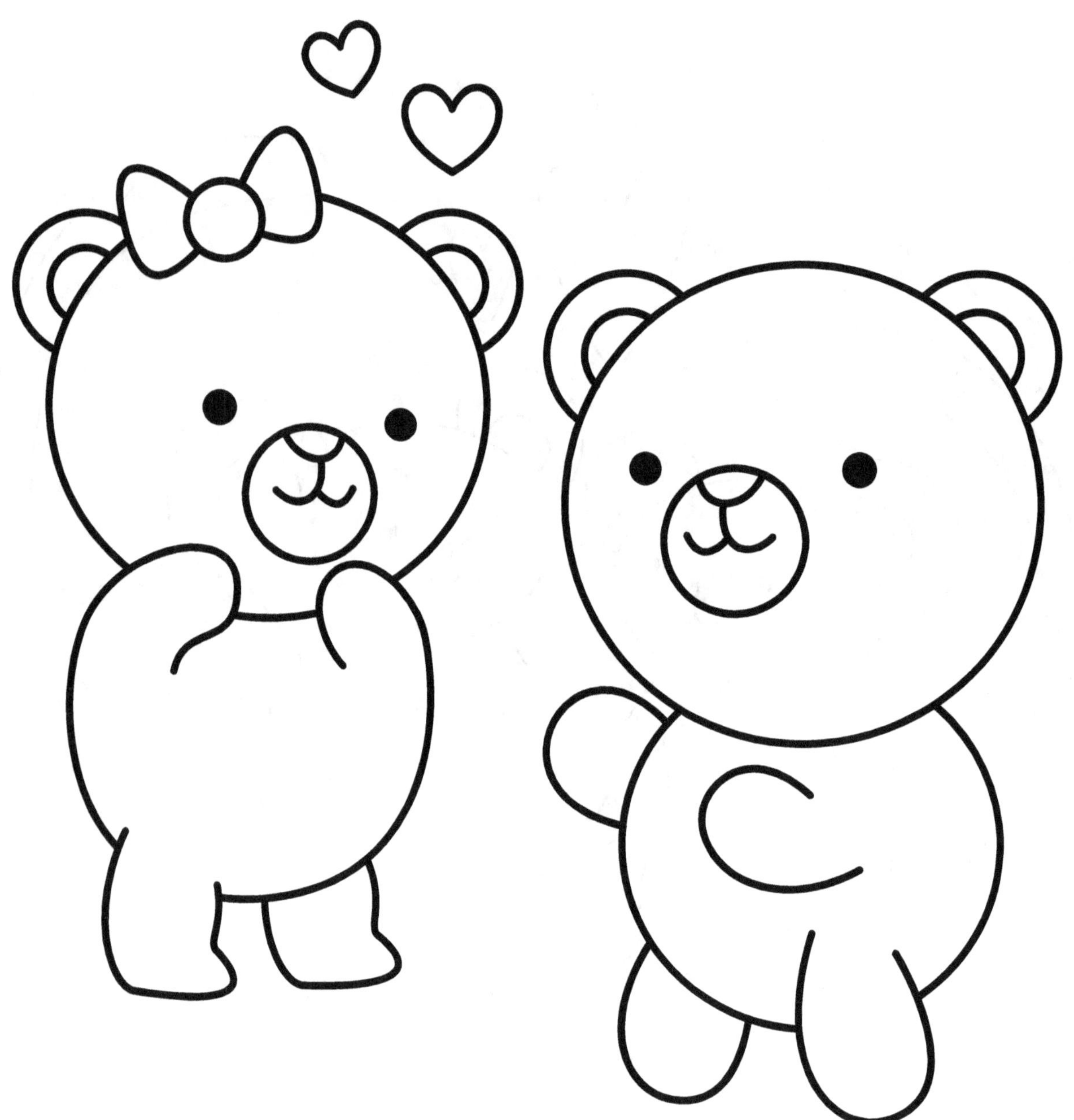

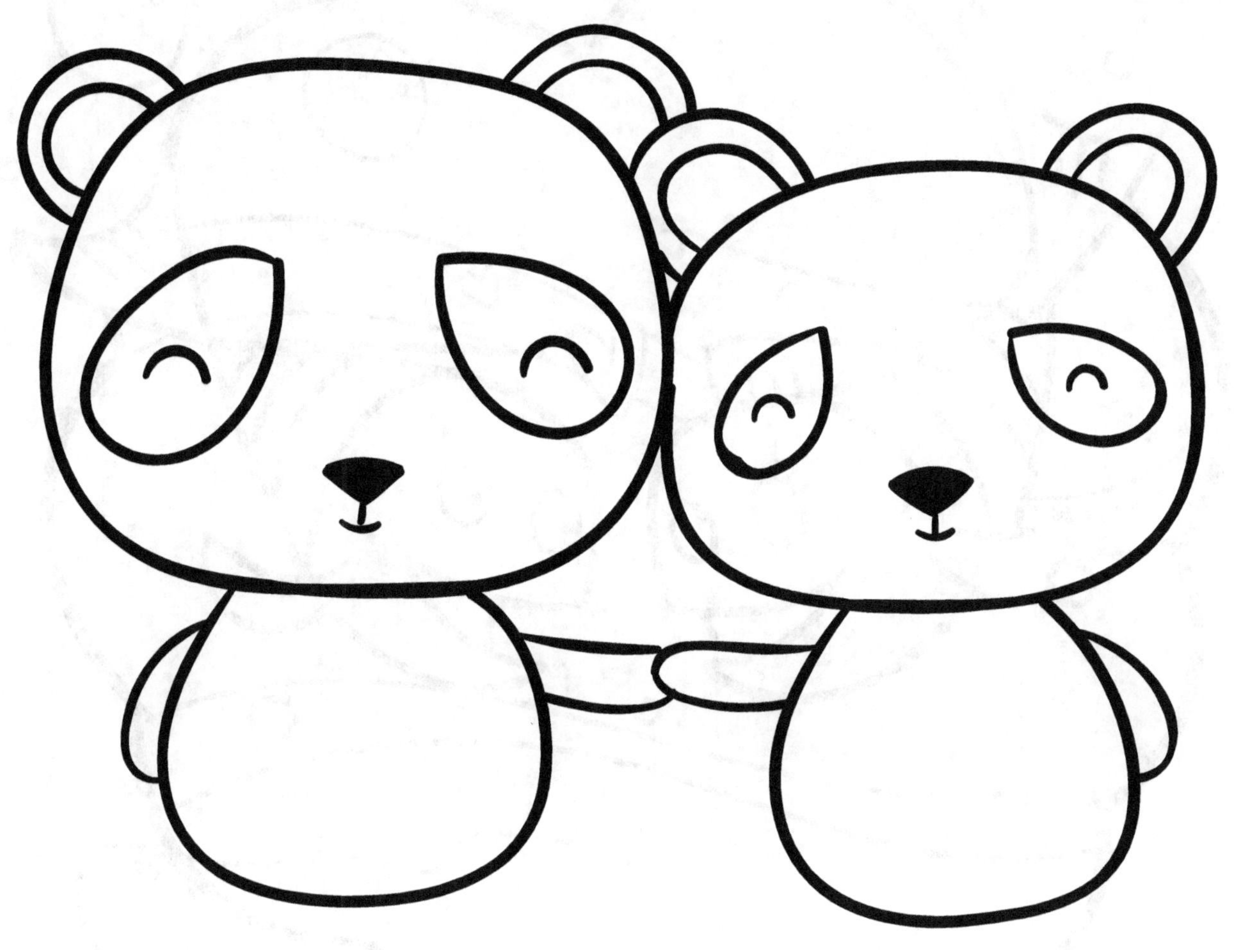

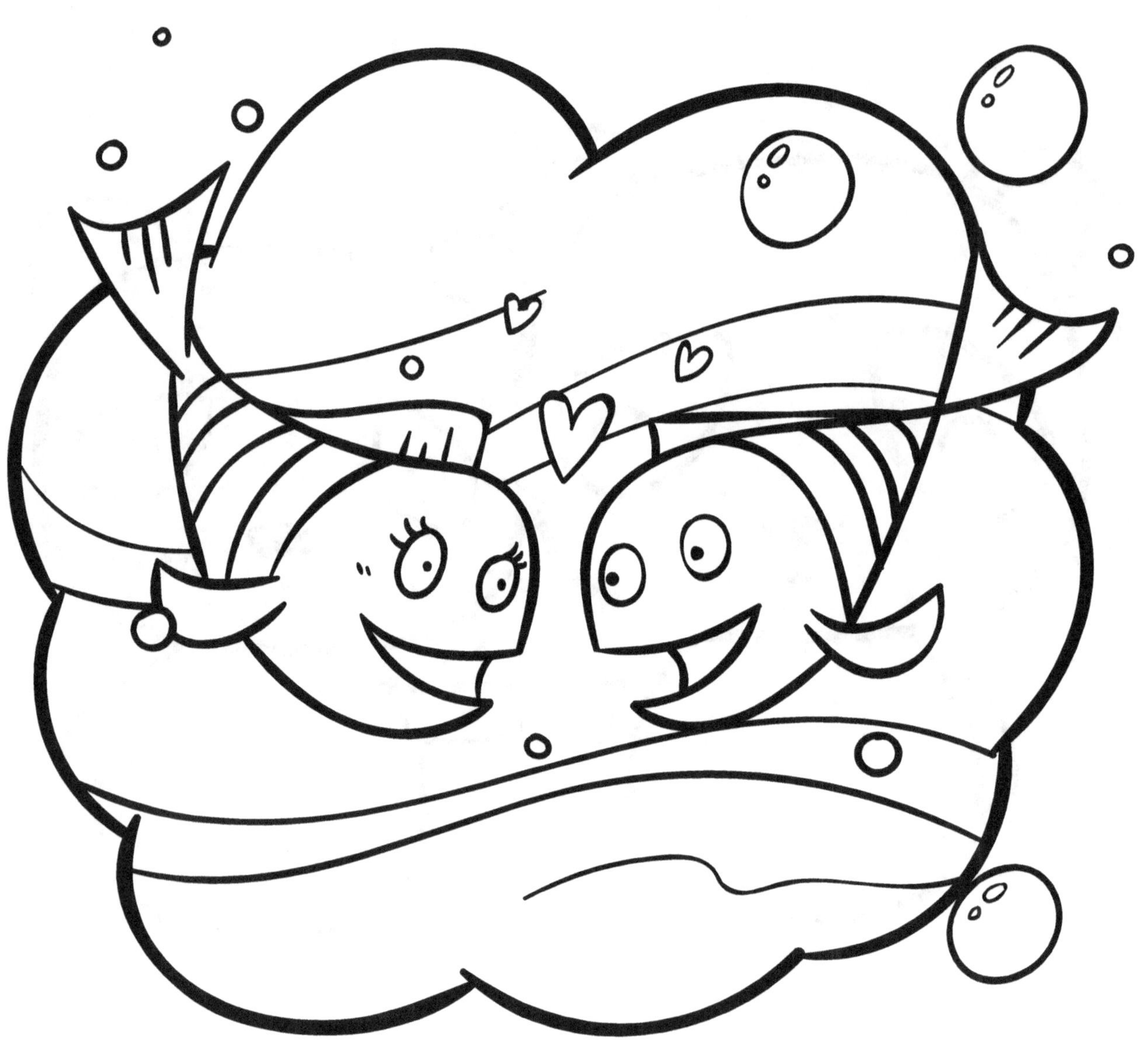

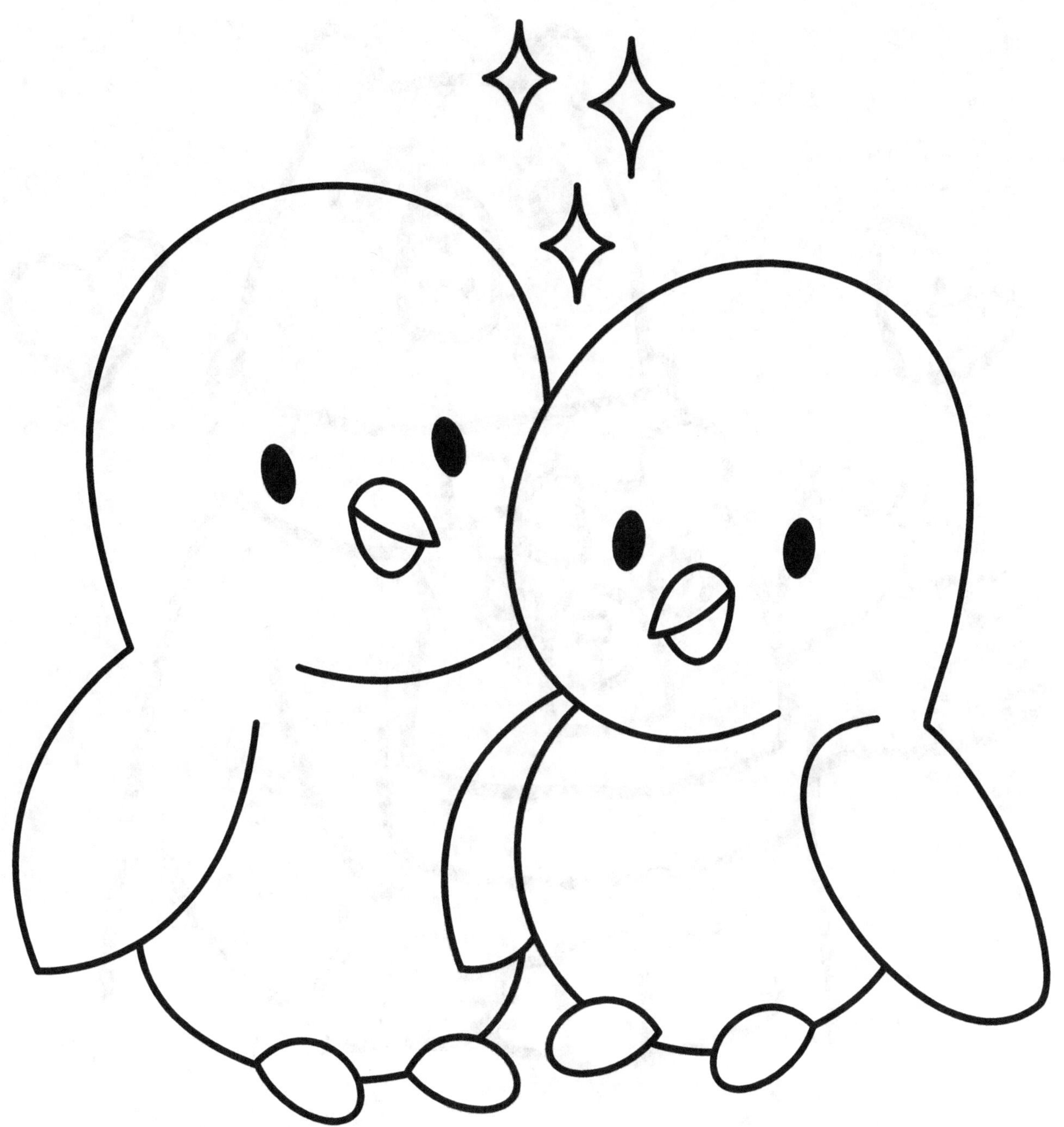

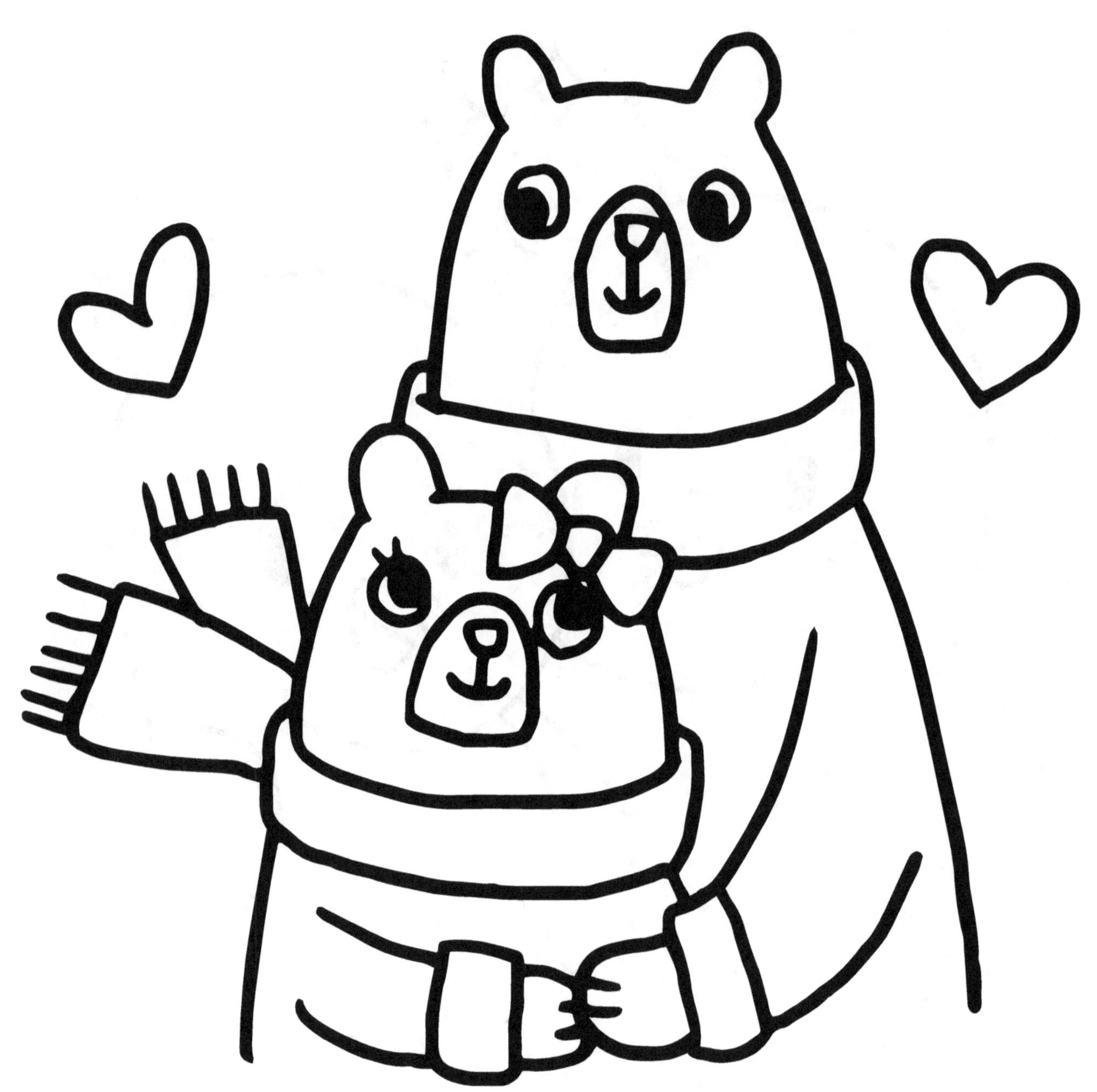

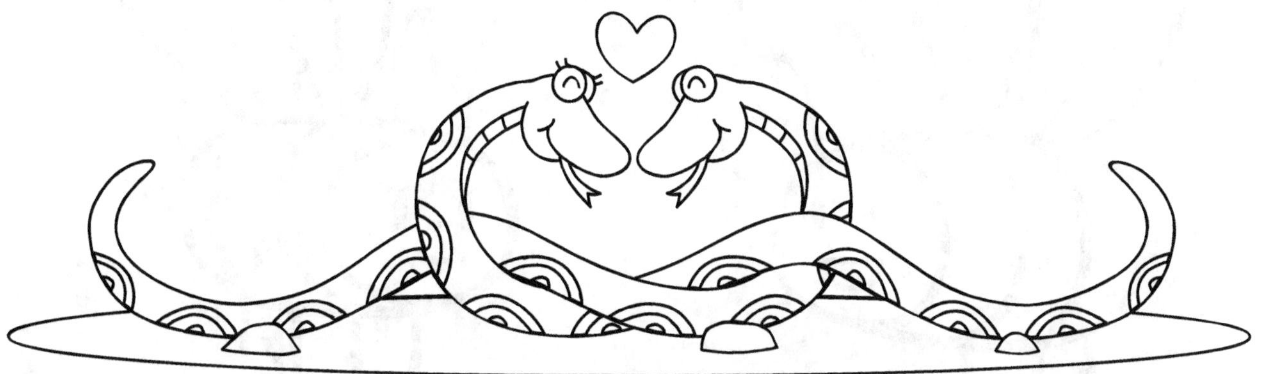

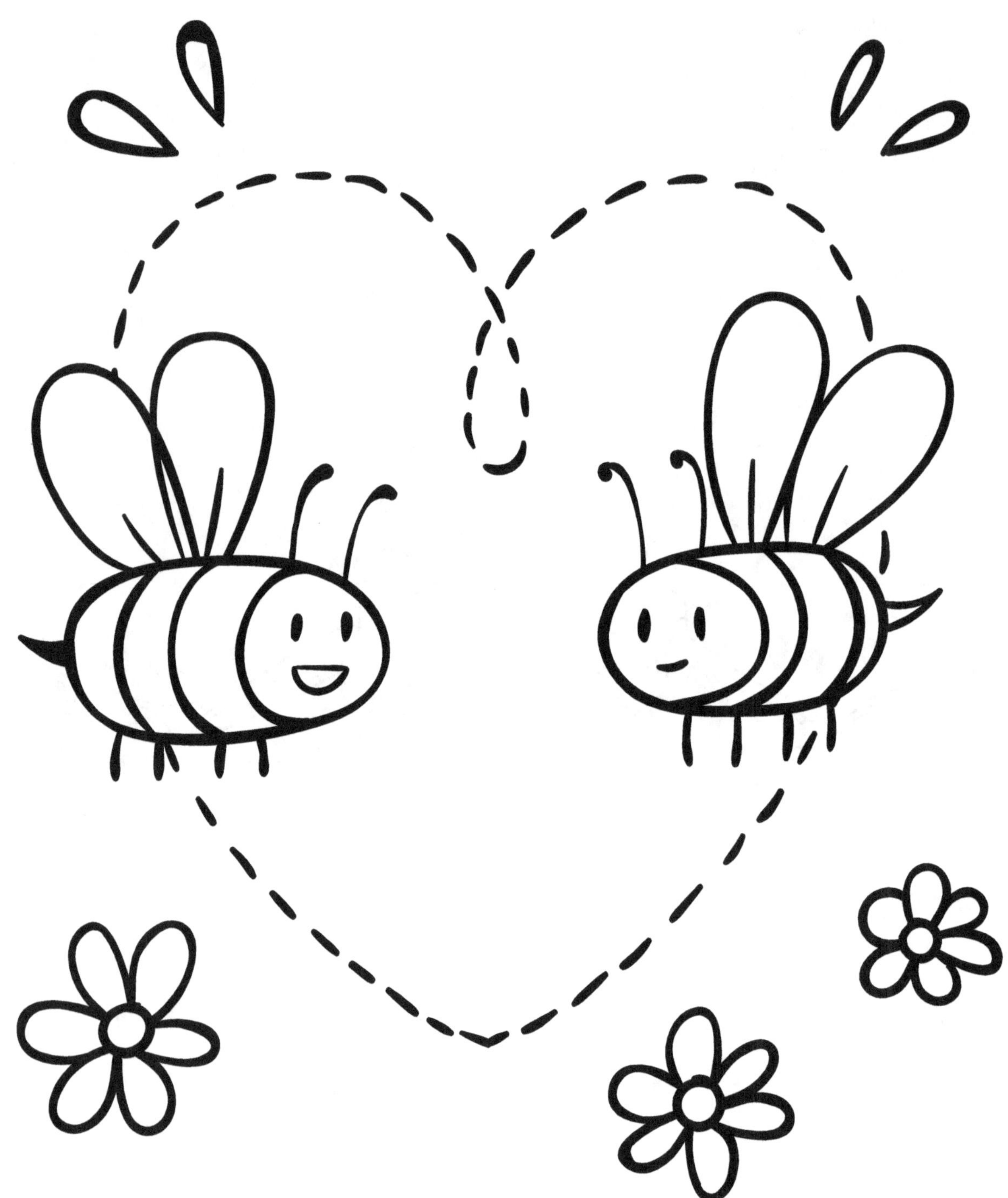

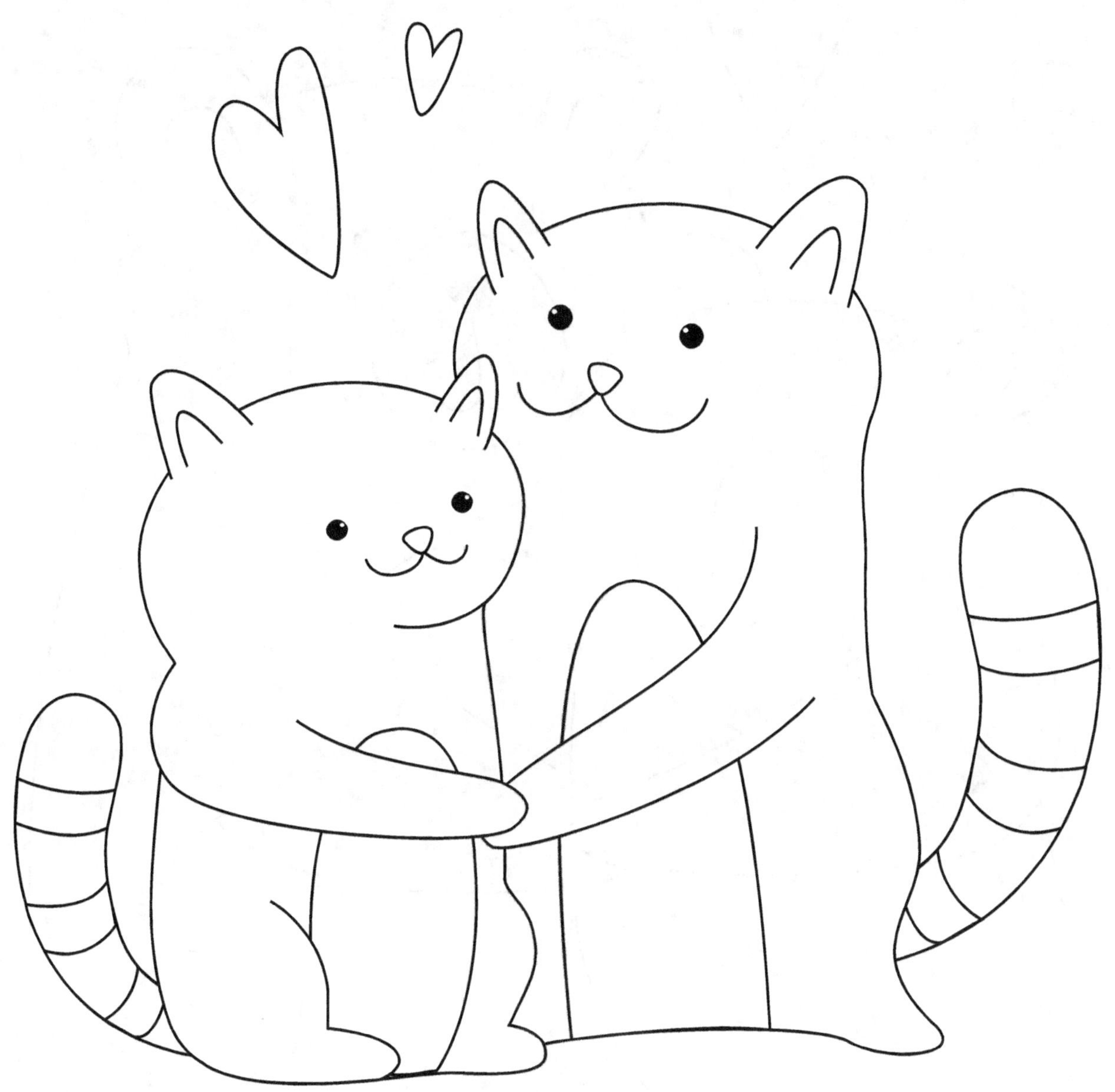

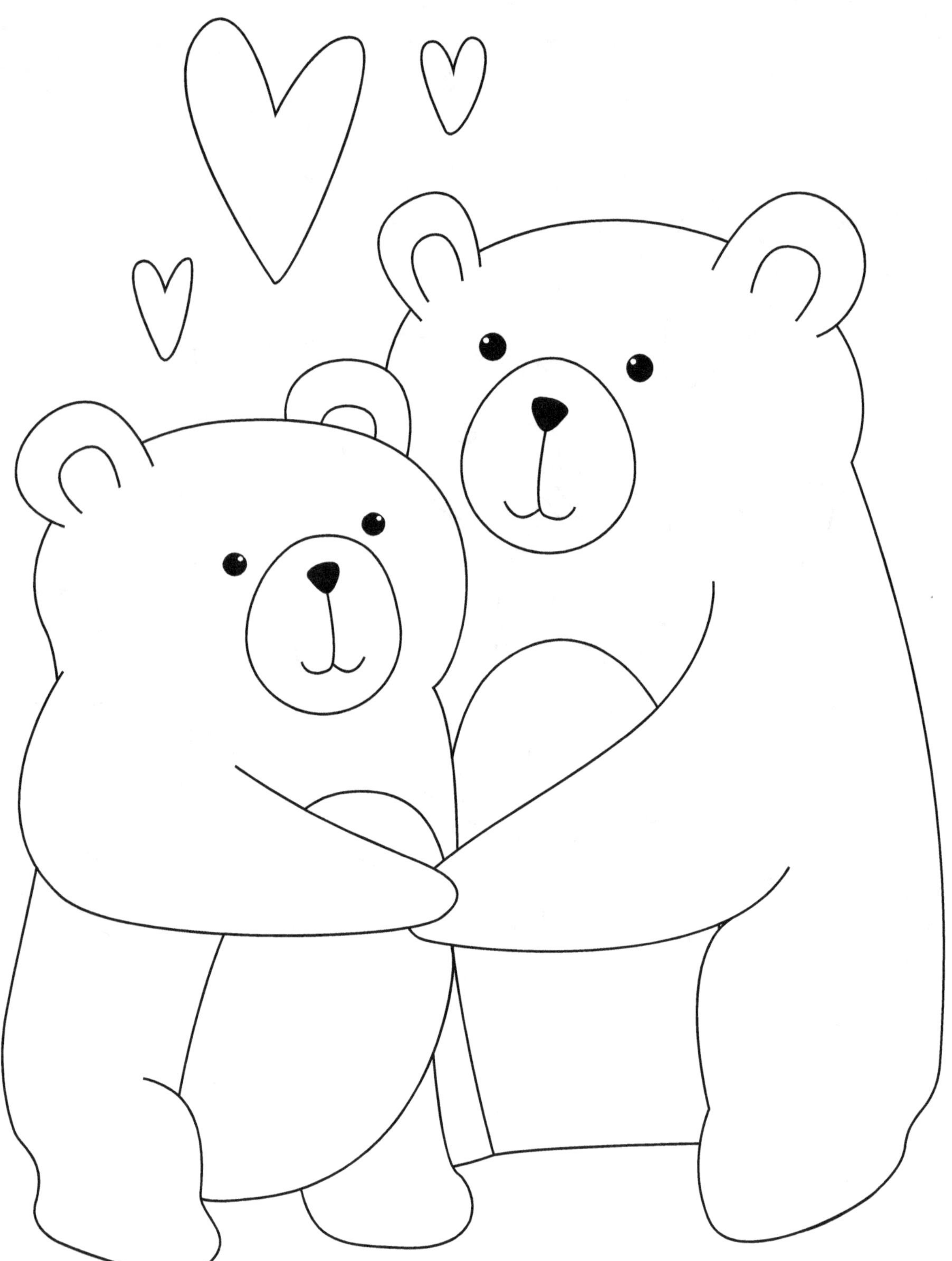

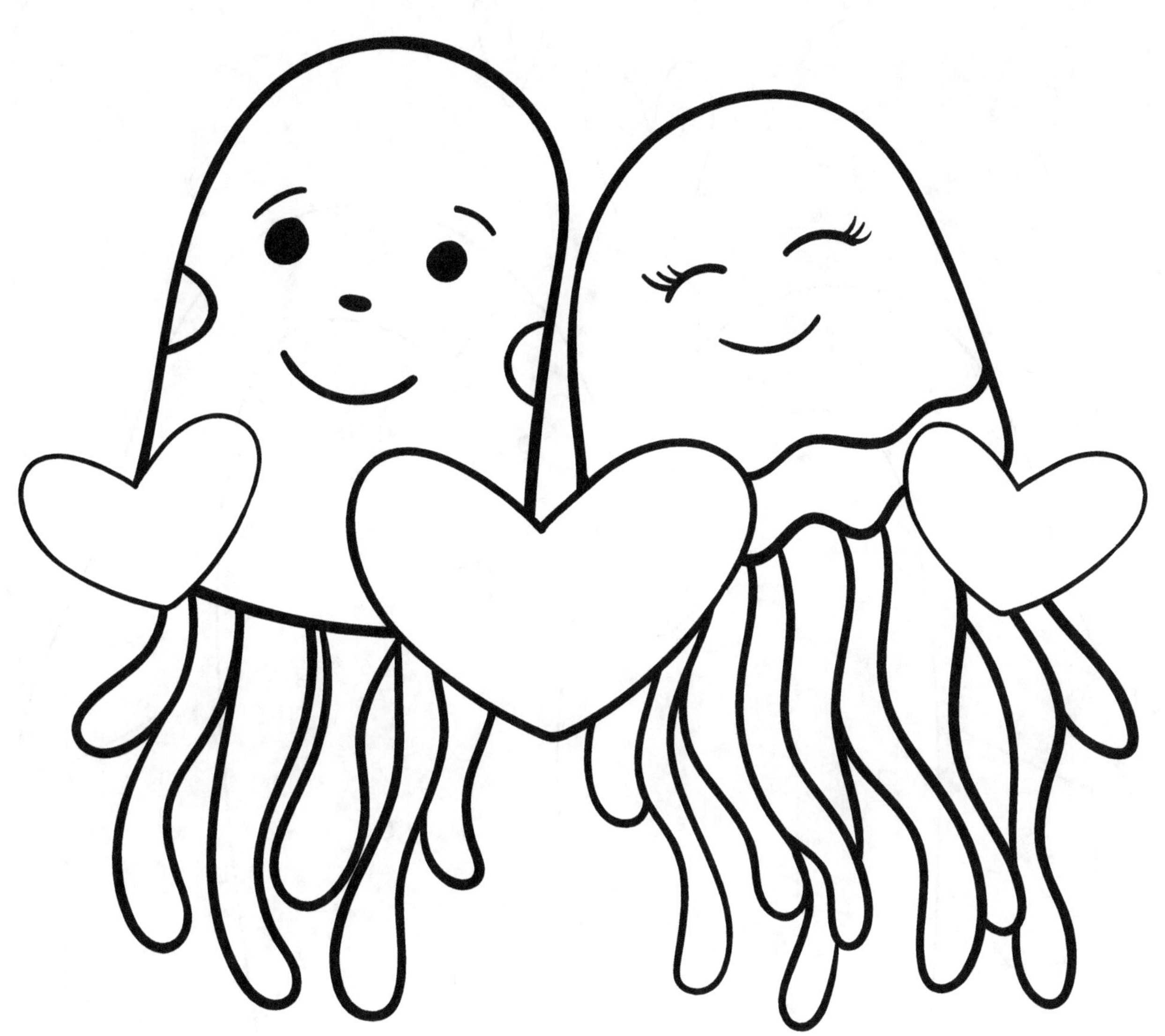

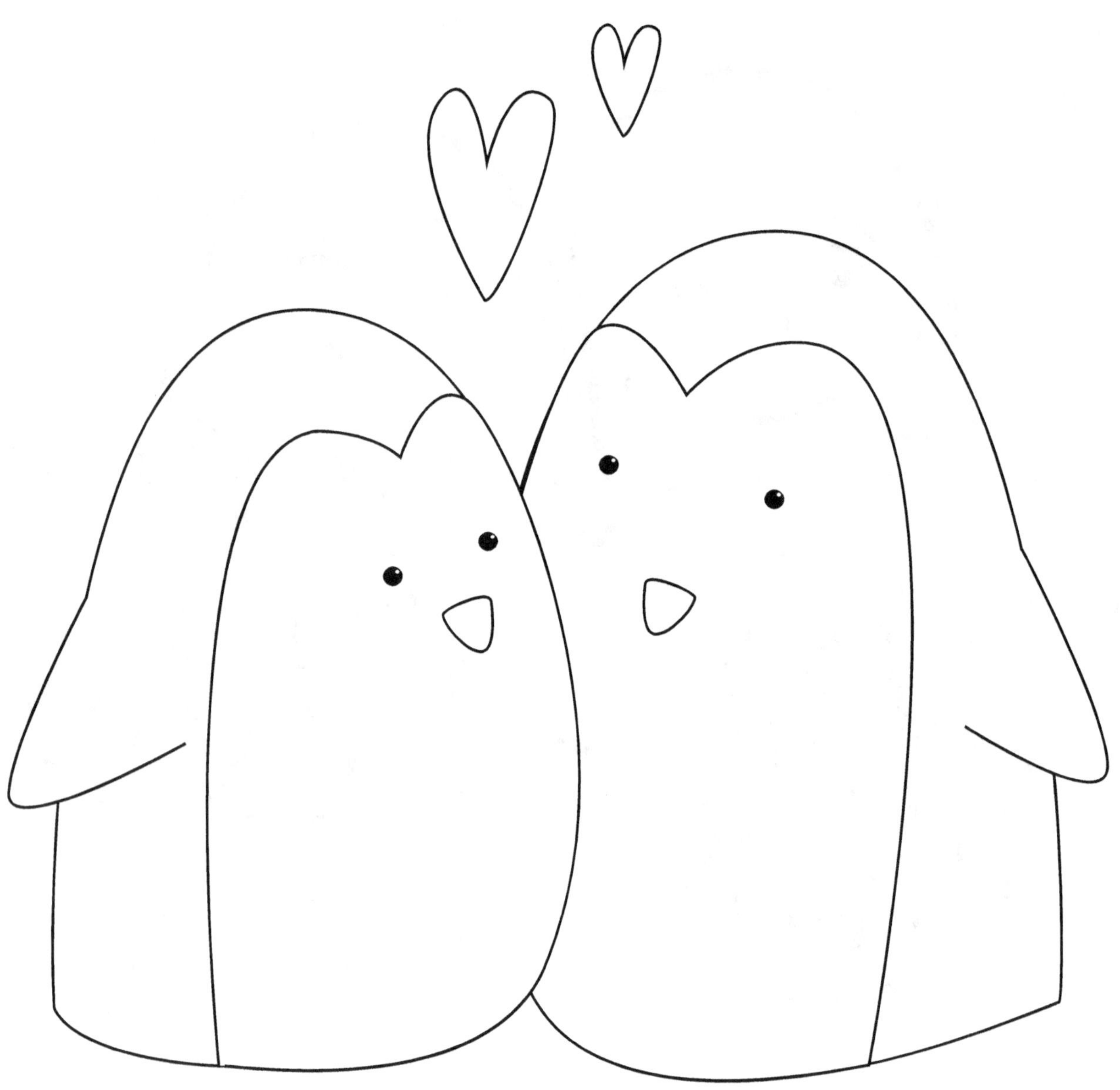

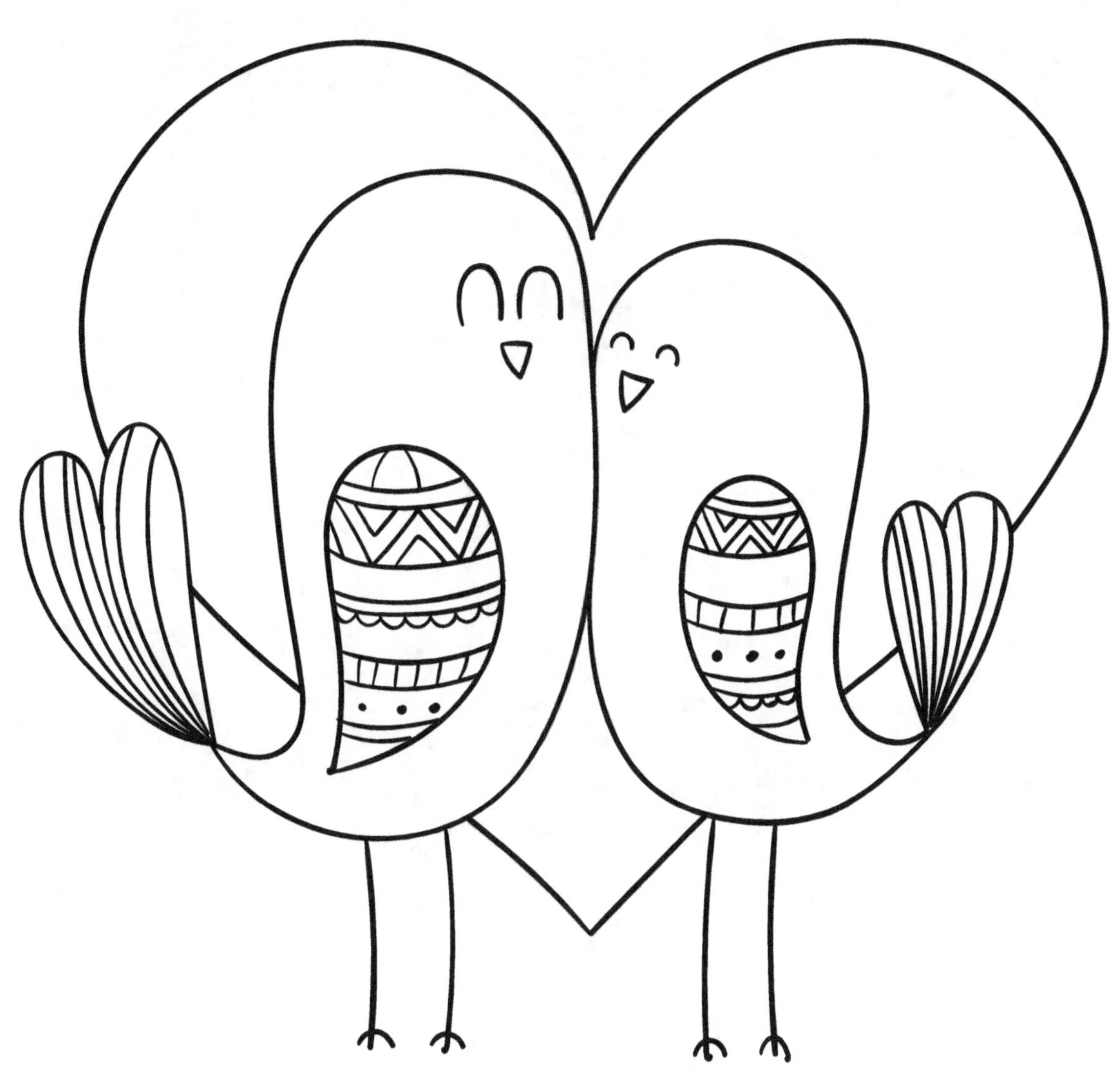

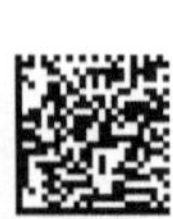